That's In The Bible?

Scripture's User-Friendly Impact on Everyday Conversation

William D. Mayo

AuthorHouse™
1663 Liberty Drive
Bloomington, IN 47403
www.authorhouse.com
Phone: 1-800-839-8640

First published by AuthorHouse 12/7/2011

ISBN: 978-1-4634-7437-9 (sc)
ISBN: 978-1-4634-7435-5 (e)
ISBN: 978-1-4634-7436-2 (dj)

Library of Congress Control Number: 2011915719

Printed in the United States of America

This book is printed on acid-free paper.

All verses are from the King James Version of the Bible unless otherwise noted.

Preface

The Bible is unquestionably one of the most widely read, translated, and published works in the history of man. Today, there are an estimated one billion Bibles in existence; and another three million copies are printed each year. Clearly, from the earliest stone tablets to Gutenberg's printing press to the present, the words of scripture have reached millions, with a profound influence on society, government, art, and language as the result.

Today, our written and verbal language is seasoned with hundreds of colorful expressions lifted directly from the pages of scripture. Newspapers quote it in headlines, advertisements use biblical quotes to lure customers, and you and I use the Bible casually in everyday speech. We will examine many such phrases in this book. Everyday expressions, voiced from the corporate boardroom to the schoolyard playground, will be presented and traced to their original biblical roots. The study of such word and phrase origins is known as etymology. Scholars in this field, called etymologists, have long recognized the influence of scripture on the vocabulary and phrasing of modern English.

I do not, however, present this book as genuine scholarly etymology. It is a layman's approach, yet I have relied on recognized research authorities when available. With some phrases, however, I have merely taken a leap of logic to support my reasoning. In either case, my purpose is not to create scholarly debate. I wrote this book to promote Bible discovery, readership, and witnessing. It is intended to illustrate the Bible as truly "user-friendly." If it succeeds toward that end, I'll concede all other argument.

****

Etymology: From the Greek words etymon, meaning "true sense," and logos, meaning "word." May this book contribute to your discovery of the true word.

William D. Mayo

Table of Contents

Introduction

User-friendly? I can well imagine your skepticism. This overused term is often met with doubt. Created by some zealous computer manufacturer, this phrase attempts to lure doubting neophytes into the computer and Internet age. "C'mon, it's *so* easy to use," they promise. Suspiciously, most cringe upon hearing it, passing it off as marketing hype. Byte, hard disk, floppy disk, processor, World Wide Web—these words sound *anything* but friendly! And there are still those holdouts who fear being ensnared in the web of technology! Quite naturally, then, when yet another "user-friendly" claim hits the street, especially related to the Bible, skepticism is understandable.

But consider those "user-friendly" claims and those strange Internet technology terms for a moment. As with anything new, comfort zones expand with exposure and practice. Today, these and many other techno-terms are the familiar language of the workplace, the school, and even the home. Despite the skeptics, the computer has not only become a household word but an increasingly popular household item. And the Internet appears to be redefining the way our world shops, learns, and even chats! Perhaps it is "user-friendly" after all.

The Bible is another common household item. And though many consider it difficult to read or understand, people actually use it every day, often quoting the Bible in friendly, casual conversations. It is, in fact, so "user-friendly," most don't even recognize they are quoting scripture. Fewer still recognize the great number of "Bible-ese" terms and phrases that have become part of our everyday colloquial vocabulary. Ironically, many of these slang expressions and phrases come verbatim from the King James Version, often maligned as the most "unfriendly" translation of all.

Truthfully, it can be difficult to comprehend some biblical passages. But, as you read on, you'll discover it contains many familiar phrases, more than you might initially expect. You will encounter a surprising number of colloquial expressions that originate from its pages, sayings you hear every day and perhaps use every day. While familiar with these phrases, it may be that you're not as comfortable with their source. As you read each one, I trust the Bible's "user-unfriendly" reputation will fade and skepticism will give way to an enthusiastic desire to search its pages.

Each phrase is offered in three sections:

Today's Phrase: Examines how the expression is used in popular form today.

Biblical Background: Explains the context and usage of the phrase during Bible times.

Bible Byte: Offers a brief "byte" of information or an application of the phrase from a spiritual perspective.

The Bible has indeed had a tremendous influence on our culture and our everyday language. It can also have a tremendous influence on you. May you become increasingly comfortable with it through daily exposure and practice. And, when you hear someone use a casual phrase contained in this book, take the opportunity to direct them to the source, the greatest book ever written—the Bible.

Apple of My Eye

Deuteronomy 32:10
Psalm 17:8
Proverbs 7:2

Today's Phrase: I'm one of those proud and doting fathers. My five children are truly God's richest blessing in my life. Though each is unique, they hold one attribute solidly in common. Each is undeniably the "apple of my eye"!

This timeworn expression has come to symbolize something prized and protected, an object of great personal value. And, though I don't "own" my children, I certainly cherish them. Several Old Testament books contain this phrase, and biblical context is identical to today's popular meaning.

Biblical Background: Deuteronomy 32:10 expresses that the Lord kept Jacob as "the apple of his eye," protecting him and guiding him through a "waste howling wilderness." In Psalms, David prays, "Keep me as the apple of the eye, hide me under the shadow of thy wings" (Psalm 17:8).

In Proverbs 7:2, wise Solomon instructs, "Keep my commandments, and live; and my law as the apple of thine eye."

Though not specifically used in Genesis, the phrase "apple of my eye" might also logically apply in the context of Eve's temptation in the Garden of Eden. Eve coveted the godly knowledge symbolized by the fruit from the tree of knowledge of good and evil. Satan seduced her into acting out her desire to possess it. The desire of her eye, or the "apple" of her eye, was that fruit which she most prized.

Clearly, similarities to today's phrase in both meaning and usage appear to be more than mere coincidence. Yet, modern etymologists suggest the phrase relates to a different "apple." Early science considered the pupil of the human eye to be a solid, globular body and likened it to an apple. Since any damage to the pupil would jeopardize the precious gift of sight, the phrase "apple of my eye" became synonymous with a possession of great worth.

Bible Byte: Does the expression "apple of my eye" come from science or scripture? It would certainly appear that a case is made for its biblical roots, but I am not out to prove that point. Only one point is important: God cherishes each individual as a valuable treasure, as the very apple of His eye. He desires that all would come unto Him. He will lead you; He will protect you under the shadow of His wings; and He will nurture you in His garden. Come into His presence, and you will be ripe with His abundance!

At the Eleventh Hour

Matthew 20:6

Today's Phrase: Americans thrive on suspense, from old vaudevillian stage plays, in which curly locked maidens narrowly escape the sinister clutches of some villainous scoundrel, to high tech movies, in which hot-shot jet jockeys engage in supersonic aerial dogfights. Seemingly, we never tire from the thrill of a last-second miraculous rescue. As the suspense mounts, we watch with eager anticipation, hoping for some dramatic rescue "at the eleventh hour" to save the day.

Hollywood has the formula down pat, but the idea is certainly not new. It's as old as an ancient scriptural record written by Matthew and spoken by Jesus. Etymologists agree that the popular saying "at the eleventh hour" originates from scripture. It is contained in one of Jesus's teaching parables. The rescue illustrated, however, is quite different.

Biblical Background: Matthew sets the stage for the parable in chapter 19. A wealthy young man, upon encountering Jesus, is saddened to hear he must relinquish his worldly riches to follow Him as one of His disciples. Christ uses the incident to emphasize that those encumbered with worldly concerns will find it difficult to make a sacrificial commitment. Simon Peter, ever the impulsive disciple, immediately proclaims, "Behold, we have forsaken all, and followed thee; what shall we have therefore?" (Matthew 19:27).

Essentially, Peter is asking Christ, "What's in it for us?" Christ responds that all who forsake the world for Him will be rewarded with everlasting life, but adds, "But many that are first shall be last; and the last shall be first" (Matthew 19:30).

Christ's parable, beginning in Matthew 20, illustrates His puzzling reply. A vineyard owner hired several laborers to work in his fields. Some workers were called early in the day; some a bit later; some at midday; and some, yet, at the very last moment or, as verse 6 states, "the eleventh hour." The twelve-hour workday ended a mere one hour later, and as wages were being paid, beginning with those hired last, the grumbling began.

Many workers who endured the heat of the day resented those laborers who had arrived at the "eleventh hour" because they received identical payment. The vineyard owner ignored their jealousy and chided them for their selfishness, for he chose to reward all workers equally, regardless of time spent in the fields. In effect, those hired first were last and those hired last were first.

Bible Byte: A beautiful lesson unfolds in this parable. God, like the vineyard owner, will reward all servants equally, not based on the amount of work done but for *faithfulness* to the task for which called. It's not the magnitude of activity, nor is it the far-reaching effects of our service that garners reward; it's the simple faithfulness of our service.

While not as dramatic as the "eleventh hour" miracles of the entertainment media, it's no less thrilling! And when the final "eleventh hour" of this world arrives, it is the only rescue that matters.

At Wit's End

Psalm 107:27

Today's Phrase: I may not have thought it at the time, but looking back, I wouldn't trade my nine years of naval service for anything. It educated me, matured me, and created a rich fabric of experience I could never replace. For three of those years, I was stationed aboard USS *Direct*, a 172-foot, wooden, oceangoing minesweeper. We used to proudly boast, amid a fleet of enormous steel-hulled vessels, we were the last of the navy's "wooden ships and iron men." And we could trade sea stories with the heartiest of sailors.

Being such a small vessel, *Direct* would bob like a cork in rough seas; but she was much more seaworthy than many of her crew. One particularly stormy night, off the coast of treacherous Cape Hatteras, gale-force winds stirred up twelve-foot seas and battered the ship relentlessly. I was on the bridge for the midwatch, from midnight to four o'clock in the morning, with a solitary sound-powered phone watchman. We hung on for life as we pitched and rolled through the blackness. Eventually, the bridge awning tore loose, and greenish ocean spray engulfed the bridge, at a height of thirty-five feet above the water line. We each tied ourselves to an immovable support for safety but were still scared to death. We were "at our wit's end," and all we could do was pray.

Psalms tells a similar "sea story," one any sailor can relate to, and one every "landlubber" should heed.

Biblical Background: "They that go down to the sea in ships, that do business in the great waters; These see the works of the LORD, and his wonders in the deep. For He commandeth, and raiseth the stormy wind, which lifteth up the waves thereof. They mount up to the heaven, they go down again to the depths: their soul is melted because of trouble. They reel to and fro, and stagger like a drunken man, and are at their wit's end" (Psalm 107:23–27).

Clearly, the psalmist knows the ways of the sea, but he also knows the way to calm a troubled soul: "Then they cry unto the LORD in their trouble, and he bringeth them out of their distresses. He maketh the storm a calm, so that the waves thereof are still. Then are they glad because they be quiet; so he bringeth them unto their desired haven" (Psalm 107:28–30).

Bible Byte: Life's trials, like a stormy sea, can likewise toss us about. With so many pressures in today's complex world, we're often driven to our "wit's end" trying to handle the stress. But we needn't steer the ship alone. There is a haven of rest; there is a solid support. Hang on to the Lord, and He will deliver you from your trouble. Before you get to your "wit's end," don't forget to call upon Him.

Basket Case

Exodus 2:3

Today's Phrase: Webster's defines a "basket case" as "a person who has all four limbs amputated." Today, a basket case can refer to any person or thing, which is incapacitated, uncoordinated, or simply helpless. This slang term reportedly originates from the use of baskets employed to carry severely war-wounded soldiers during the First World War. The book of Exodus however, suggests a different possibility.

Biblical Background: Pharaoh, king of Egypt, was concerned with the growing Israelite population. He feared their increased strength and, therefore, ordered the murder of all new male children born to Hebrew slaves. Newborn sons were to be thrown into the river and drowned, but newborn daughters could be spared. With this plan, Pharaoh would prevent the buildup of an organized resistance among the Israelite people by eliminating a whole generation of potential soldiers.

Chapter 2 details the account of a young Levite girl who bore a son and, in defiance of Pharaoh's decree, hid him three months. Her love was great, and she risked her own life to save his. She prepared a basket of reeds and slime, placed her son within it, and set it adrift among the bulrush reeds lining the riverbank. Pharaoh's own daughter soon discovered the basket and felt compassion for the child. She arranged for his care and eventual adoption into the very household of Pharaoh. Though the young Levite mother could not have known, this was no chance encounter. God intervened, leaving nothing to chance. His plan was perfect. The child's mother put her trust in God and was rewarded. Not only was her son's life spared, but she was also chosen by Pharaoh's daughter to nurture and care for this newly adopted child in Pharaoh's house.

Bible Byte: The child in this familiar story is Moses, destined to become one of God's greatest servants. Yet, when first discovered, he is a totally helpless, defenseless "basket case." The similar meaning for basket case today is compelling evidence of its biblical origin. But the lesson from his mother's faith is even more compelling.

God oversees the helpless and rewards those who seek and trust in Him. His plan is perfected in our weakness. Though we may be a "basket case" today, He has a wonderful plan for our nurture and growth into effective service for Him tomorrow. Don't waste another day. Let God carry you in the "basket" of His love. He can turn the helpless into the hopeful.

Birds of a Feather

Ecclesiasticus 27:9 (Apocrypha)

Today's Phrase: As a youngster, I used to run around with my best friend, Paul. We went everywhere together. We dressed the same, wore our crew cuts the same (how else?), and even tried to talk the same way. My father used to say to us, "You boys sure are 'birds of a feather.'"

"Yeah, we sure do flock together!" we shouted happily. Little did I realize this old phrase comes from ancient scripture, more specifically, the apocryphal book of Ecclesiasticus.

Biblical Background: Christian scriptures are normally considered to be only the canonized books of the Old and New Testaments. Thus far, we've only examined phrases contained in these sections. But the Protestant Apocrypha, comprised of many early Christian writings, has also impacted our colloquial language.

Apocryphal books were included in the Septuagint (a pre-Christian Greek version of the Jewish scripture) and the Vulgate (a Latin version of the Bible adopted by the Roman Catholic Church). For the most part, the writings have been excluded from the Protestant canon. Still, many Protestant Bibles are published containing this section.

The popular expression "birds of a feather" is traceable to the apocryphal book of Ecclesiasticus. The Cloverdale translation of the Bible (1535 AD) records in Ecclesiasticus, "Birds roost with their own kind" (Ecclesiasticus 27:9).

Obviously, some clever phrasing has occurred over the years resulting in the modern rhyming expression; but etymological sources agree that today's expression originates from this scripture. Usage today relates more to behavior than appearance, however. In other words, the "feather" relates to how one acts, not how one looks. All blond-haired, blue-eyed people are less likely to "flock" together than would, for example, troublemakers with troublemakers. (And I'm not implying Paul and I were either.) The phrase has colloquially evolved into an axiom for social behavior.

Unfortunately, today we frequently use this expression as an excuse or in acceptance for poor behavior. We might witness some rowdy, obnoxious group at a sporting event and dismiss it indifferently with a shrug: "Oh well, birds of a feather …"

Bible Byte: Like so many phrases we've examined, today's expression is distanced from its original intent. Reading further in Ecclesiasticus we note, "Truth comes back to those who practice it."

The emphasis in context of the entire verse is quite different. Scripture doesn't politely dismiss wrongdoing with a shrug. The emphasis intended is clearly on doing what is right.

Birds of a feather do flock together, right with right and wrong with wrong. Which flock do you roost with? Jesus wants to know.

Broke the Law

Exodus 32:19

Today's Phrase: One of my kids asked recently if I'd ever broken the law. I squirmed a bit as I considered my answer, but then admitted I'd experienced a few "run-ins" with the law thanks to our traffic courts.

Retrospectively, I'm glad my son asked that question. He piqued my curiosity about the origin for the phrase "broke the law." I didn't find any supporting sources to corroborate my suspicion of its biblical origin but, likewise, found no contradiction. A familiar Old Testament story is the basis for my assumption.

Biblical Background: Most are familiar with God's Old Testament law, referred to as the Ten Commandments. Moses actually received these instructions directly from God while on Mount Sinai. Exodus reveals that God gave Moses "tables of stone and a law and commandments" (Exodus 24:12).

It also describes that these laws were "written with the finger of God" (Exodus 31:18).

A fascinating story unfolds as we examine when and how these first laws were "broken."

Chapter 32 begins with the Israelites' tiring from waiting for Moses to return from Mount Sinai. He had been gone for almost forty days at this point, and the people were weary and restless. In rebellion, the people fashioned a golden calf and, with a reckless abandon, turned from God to feast and party in honor of their new idol. (Remember, the Israelites had been in captivity in Egypt over four hundred years and had been taught idolatry by the Egyptians.)

God became very angry, promising Moses in verses 7–10 that He would destroy the people for their wickedness. Moses returned to the camp, amazed with the corruption he discovers: the golden calf, the idol worship, and the reckless and riotous behavior of the people. In a fury, Moses threw the stone tablets to the ground, breaking God's laws into pieces.

Judgment was swift. Moses called for repentance and separated those willing to return to the Lord. Tragically, three thousand men were put to death in judgment for blasphemy. Moses returned to the mountain to confess the sin of his people and to intercede for the Israelite nation.

In chapter 34, the tablets of stone were again created and the Ten Commandments were written upon them. Although the original laws were "broken," God's law remained intact.

Bible Byte: Today we have far more laws than any two stone tablets could contain. Myriad volumes of laws and ordinances exist. But these laws, as good as they seem, are broken every day. That shouldn't surprise us, for just as before, the law doesn't prevent sin; it merely measures it. One of the Ten Commandments is "Thou shalt have no other gods before me." That law didn't keep the Israelites free from idolatry, but it was the standard by which they were judged.

We, too, will one day be judged. But just as Moses interceded for his people, Christ intercedes for us. Remember, the law will not save you. In fact, it cannot save you despite your most noble effort to be "law-abiding." It is *sin* in our lives that must be broken. Only then can God put His law in our hearts and our lives back together.

Blind Leading the Blind

Matthew 15:14

Today's Phrase: One commodity mankind eagerly gives away is advice. It flows freely and oftentimes frivolously. Talk radio has made a business of it, and the popularity of nationally syndicated advice programs belies the apparent insatiable thirst we have for the counsel of strangers.

While many of these radio advice programs are entertaining, it's tragic, if not pathetic, to consider that an audience of thousands intimately eavesdrops on the most personal problems of others. Background music and commercial cues are laced throughout the "sage counsel" in clever choreography; but the content is conspicuously void of any spiritual perspective. It has often struck me that "the blind are leading the blind." Matthew 15:14 is the biblical root for this popular expression.

Biblical Background: Jesus despised the pretentious religion of the Pharisees, observing that their outward piety and ceremonious ritual missed the heart of His message. Man is inwardly defiled, not outwardly. Man requires spiritual cleansing and purification, not external "window dressing."

Oh, the Pharisees looked the part all right. Their outward appearance and behavior mirrored the law as a perfect reflection. But they neglected spiritual issues and motive. Christ, referring to the Pharisees said, "They be blind leaders of the blind. And if the blind lead the blind, both shall fall into the ditch" (Matthew 15:14).

Bible Byte: Yes, in Jesus's time, just as today, free advice abounded. But although it is "free," it is not without price. In the Pharisees' world, they taught strict adherence to legalistic ritual and traditions but ignored the inward evils of pride, false pretense, and true motive. Those who followed blindly paid a high price.

Today's world also freely offers its counsel. The radio airwaves are a mere sampling of the alternatives, from humanism to the power of positive thinking. But today's "free advice" also has a price attached. While inappropriate to condemn it all, it's important to recognize the world has some treacherously deep ditches. You're only truly safe when you can trust whom you're following. Keep your eyes on Christ. When He's in the lead of your life, the footing will be safe and sure.

Burning the Midnight Oil

Matthew 25:1–13

Today's Phrase: Anyone who's ever remodeled an old house can relate to the phrase "burning the midnight oil." After packing in a full day's work, plus a full evening schedule of supper, supervising kid's homework, and chauffeuring for special events, there's simply precious little time left, not to mention very little energy. Still, many times I find myself engrossed in a project well into the wee hours of the morning. Of course, the next day at work is miserable. And, after a steady week's diet of this pace, the circles under my eyes give me away. I'm greeted knowingly with an arched brow, "Burning the midnight oil, again, huh?" This may be said in an understanding tone, but the common implication is, "It's catching up to you, and it's pretty foolish."

Matthew's gospel account offers another example when foolishly "burning the midnight oil" met with inescapable consequence. It's also a revealing portrait of our need for spiritual preparedness.

Biblical Background: This phrase clearly originates within the context of Christ's parable of the ten virgins. Christ likened the kingdom of heaven "unto ten virgins, which took their lamps, and went forth to meet the bridegroom. And five of them were wise, and five were foolish. They that were foolish took their lamps, and took no oil with them: But the wise took oil in their vessels with their lamps. While the bridegroom tarried, they all slumbered and slept. And at midnight there was a cry made, Behold, the bridegroom cometh; go ye out to meet him.

Then all those virgins arose, and trimmed their lamps. And the foolish said unto the wise, Give us of your oil; for our lamps are gone out" (Matthew 25:1–8).

Foolishly, they had already burned their "midnight oil" and had not brought any reserves. They were not ready, were ill prepared, and their foolishness caught up with them.

"But the wise answered, saying, Not so; lest there be not enough for us and you: but go ye rather to them that sell, and buy for yourselves. And while they went to buy, the bridegroom came; and they that were ready went in with him to the marriage: and the door was shut. Afterward came also the other virgins, saying, Lord, Lord, open to us. But he answered and said, Verily I say unto you, I know you not" (Matthew 25:9–12).

Bible Byte: The message is simple and beautifully clear. Be prepared. Christ will return for His "bride," the church. And spiritually speaking, "burning the midnight oil" carries a price we cannot afford. Five of ten virgins paid that price. They were shut out from the marriage feast. Christ sounds a clear warning of this parable's meaning in verse 13: "Watch therefore, for ye know neither the day nor the hour wherein the Son of man cometh" (Matthew 25:13).

After a few days' rest, I can usually overcome the physical toll my midnight projects extract; but spiritually, there will be no second chance, no opportunity for rest, and no chance for recovery. Christ, the Bridegroom of the church, is coming soon. Take your rest in Him now and prepare yourself for His coming!

Caught in the Act

John 8:4

Today's Phrase: We can all undoubtedly recall embarrassing youthful memories when we were "caught in the act" of some inappropriate behavior. These memories range from an innocent episode of "snitching" Mom's fresh-baked cookies to some more mischievous events I'd rather not admit. In any case, the phrase "caught in the act" meant there were no escape, no clever excuses, and no denials. It was a definite "Gotcha!" The Gospel of John presents an interesting episode from which we've derived today's popular expression, "caught in the act."

Biblical Background: As Jesus's popularity increased, the scribes and Pharisees continually tried to trip Him up in situations that would cause Him to contradict the restrictive web of Mosaic laws. In John 8:3, in the midst of a crowded temple gathering, an adulterous woman was brought before Him. This woman was not merely alleged of the crime of adultery, but her accusers were certain she was guilty of a grievous offense: "Master, this woman was taken in adultery, in the very act" (John 8:4).

She could offer no denial and no excuse. There were no doubts. The Pharisees felt they could snare Jesus by forcing Him to confront the reality of her sin with condemnation. Certainly, He could not forgive such a grievous sin in the midst of all these witnesses. They taunted Christ with the dilemma of the law: "Now Moses in the law commanded us, that such should be stoned: but what sayest thou?" (John 8:5).

Jesus sat silently, head down, and wrote on the ground with His finger as if He didn't hear them. They persisted. Finally, Jesus lifted His head, saying, "He that is without sin among you, let him first cast a stone at her" (John 8:7).

The self-righteous Pharisees had met their match. They succeeded in creating a confrontation to be sure, but it was not with Jesus. They were confronted by their own guilt and guilty conscience. They quietly retreated, one by one, leaving only the humiliated woman with the Lord. No doubt surrounded her guilt; but now, neither did man's condemnation surround her. Jesus refused to condemn her for her obvious sin. And, more importantly, she received Christ's forgiveness. She fades from scripture as a forgiven soul with Christ's charge to "Go and sin no more."

Bible Byte: When we are confronted with our sin, "caught in the very act," we, too, have no excuse. But, just as this adulterous woman, if we put our trust in Jesus and confess to Him, our accusers will quietly disappear. We'll be left alone, in the loving forgiveness and acceptance of the Lord Jesus Christ.

Caught Between the Devil and the Deep Blue Sea

Exodus 14:2–3

Today's Phrase: There are many colloquialisms that describe being caught in a difficult situation. For example, "that's a tough spot to be in," "the lesser of two evils," "between a rock and a hard spot," "damned if you do, damned if you don't," "six of one, half a dozen of another," and, there is my favorite, "caught between the devil and the deep blue sea." It's my favorite because it relates the miraculous escape of the children of Israel from slavery under Egypt's Pharaoh. And, because it's the only expression which, when examined in context, illustrates hope. The others leave you hanging gloomily, without promise or prospect. The ancient Exodus story reveals that through God's hand, a ray of hope is always near.

Biblical Background: The children of Israel were captive in Egypt for 430 years before the Lord called them out of bondage at Moses' hand. God went before them "by day in a pillar of a cloud … and by night in a pillar of fire" (Exodus 13:21), leading them through the wilderness toward the Red Sea. Pharaoh, his heart hardened at the plagues that befell Egypt, began to reconsider his decision to let the Israelites go free. He chose to follow them, knowing he could overtake them and again enslave Israel's people. God, knowing Pharaoh's heart, directed Moses to camp by the great sea.

"For Pharaoh will say of the children of Israel, They are entangled in the land, the wilderness hath shut them in" (Exodus 14:3). With Pharaoh at their heels and the Red Sea before them, they were "caught between the devil and the deep blue sea."

"And when Pharaoh drew nigh, the children of Israel lifted up their eyes, and, behold, the Egyptians marched after them; and they were sore afraid: and the children of Israel cried out unto the LORD" (Exodus 14:10).

The miracle of the parting sea is well known. As God directed, Moses stretched his rod before the great waters and they divided. The children of Israel marched through on dry ground with a wall of sea on either side. As the Egyptians followed, again Moses stretched forth his hands, and the deep blue sea swallowed up Pharaoh's army.

"Thus the LORD saved Israel that day out of the hand of the Egyptians; and Israel saw the Egyptians dead upon the sea shore. And Israel saw that great work which the LORD did upon the Egyptians: and the people feared the LORD, and believed the LORD" (Exodus 14:30–31).

Bible Byte: Satan likes to back us into corners. And his darkness can so overshadow the mind that we fail to see any ray of hope. He wants us to give up. He wants us to give in. He wants to overtake us and enslave us to the powers of sin. But there is hope. There is an escape. Just as the children of Israel did, we must cry unto the Lord. You may feel "caught between the devil and the deep blue sea," but Christ is a safe and sure life preserver. Jump in and hold fast to Him, and He'll bring you safely to the other shore, the promised land.

Crystal Clear

Revelation 21:11
Revelation 22:1

Today's Phrase: Kids are amazing. They have an uncanny ability to hear selectively. They listen especially well to things like "Yes, you can sleep over at Billy's house," or "Sure, you can go to the movies." But, they don't do so well with directions, such as "Pick up your room," or "Don't forget to brush your teeth." Because of this tendency, parents have to be very clear about the rules of the game. "Sure, you can go to the movies, as soon as your room is picked up." There is not much chance to misinterpret that one. Still, knowing that kids can also tune out the conditions, every parent has probably used the phrase "Is that crystal clear?"

John's book of Revelation, perhaps universally considered the most difficult Bible prophecy to understand, ironically originates the phrase "crystal clear."

Biblical Background: Revelation is the final book in the Bible. In its final chapter, John, writing of the vision given to him by God, describes the New Jerusalem. It is a holy city, built by God, and one that "descends out of heaven from God" (Revelation 21:10).

Chapters 20 and 21 describe in vivid detail the city: twelve gates of pearl, its foundation and walls made of precious gemstones, and its streets of pure gold. Chapter 22 provides this additional description: "And he shewed me a pure river of water of life, clear as crystal, proceeding out of the throne of God and of the Lamb" (Revelation 22:1).

This water of life was "crystal clear," implying no impurities, no pollution, and no imperfection. And its source was the throne of God. It can't get any clearer than that, which is most probably what led to our colloquial meaning today. Is that "crystal clear"? If it is, then there's no mistake about it. It's both "crystal clear" and "perfectly clear," just as the source of New Jerusalem's river of the water of life was perfect.

Bible Byte: In John's gospel, Christ, speaking to the Samaritan woman at the well, says, "Whosoever drinketh of the water that I shall give him shall never thirst; but the water that I shall give him shall be in him a well of water springing up into everlasting life" (John 4:14).

Make no mistake about it. Christ is the way to life eternal. And He wants to give that living water to you. His word makes that "crystal clear."

Come Out of the Closet

Matthew 6:6

Today's Phrase: To "come out of the closet" is to publicly expose that which is normally held closely private or secluded. You might hear an embarrassed admission to discover a "closet smoker" or "closet drinker." "Coming out of the closet" brings these habits into the open. Yet, it might surprise some that New Testament scriptures actually *recommend* a certain type of "closet behavior." However, the practice prescribed was intended to avoid sin, not hide in secrecy.

Biblical Background: Matthew 6 reveals Christ's disgust with the outward religion exhibited by the Pharisees. He condemned their phony piety, pretentious prayers, and personal pride. He knew their prayers were vainly repetitious, filled with feigned humility. Their motives were to direct men's admiration toward themselves, not God. He admonished those assembled to "enter into thy closet … shut thy door, pray to thy Father which is in secret; and thy Father which seeth in secret shall reward thee openly" (Matthew 6:6). What a contrast with the Pharisees' hypocritical show. Christ's command to enter the closet meant, "Don't boast or seek man's public approval, rather seek to privately, personally please God."

Bible Byte: The world today has far too many "open closets." The clutter is spilling out everywhere. In our "anything goes" morality, social behavior traditionally viewed as degenerate and unacceptable is now openly paraded in public view. Innocuously labeled "alternative lifestyles" by the liberal media, we are apparently expected to tolerantly embrace the deviant behavior of homosexuals and transvestites. Similarly, we are to celebrate the diverse radical ideologies of racial supremacists or Satan worshippers in praise of free speech. Myriad prurient interests have "come out of the closet" openly, defiantly, and even arrogantly, while conservative moral values are pinched and squeezed.

Putting these social diseases back into the closet's private realm doesn't lessen their evil, but limited social exposure can stave off public acceptance of such aberrant behavior as "normal." What is truly necessary is a return to the closet as Christ encouraged, not to hide our sins but to prayerfully confess them.

Can't Take it with You

Ecclesiastes 5:15

Today's Phrase: The rock star Madonna had a popular song in recent years called "Material Girl." Its lyrics sing of the desire for things, and truly, the world operates in sync with her standard. The pursuit of material possessions is frenzied, especially among the so-called yuppie generation. Their philosophy seems to be "spend it all; you can't take it with you." Solomon's writing in Ecclesiastes is the origin for today's phrase.

Biblical Background: Solomon is perhaps best remembered for his godly wisdom, yet in Ecclesiastes he writes of his experiences at a time when he was separated from God. This separation occurred during Solomon's futile search for life's purpose apart from God. He experimented with everything "under the sun" vainly hoping to obtain fulfillment in life without God. Whether Philosophy, science, physical pleasures, materialism, egotism, religion, or the pursuit of wealth, Solomon writes from personal experience about them all and about the futility of each to fill the void created by man's separation from God.

Many popular expressions can be traced to Solomon's ecclesiastical writings: "everything under the sun," (Ecclesiastes 1:3), "nothing new under the sun," (Ecclesiastes 1:9), "eat, drink, and be merry," (Ecclesiastes 8:15), as well as many others we'll examine later.

Though these expressions are scriptural, it's dangerous to lift them out of context to support an inappropriate philosophy for life. For example, chapter 8 offers this popular morsel: "Because a man hath no better thing under the sun, than to eat, and to drink, and to be merry" (Ecclesiastes 8:15). Obviously, many today could latch onto this to rationalize a "grab the gusto" philosophy. But such excerpts taken out of context often lead to misinterpretation. Solomon's ultimate conclusions are much different.

Such is the case with the popular phrase "you can't take it with you." Today, society relies on this philosophy for a license to live selfishly, irresponsibly, and frivolously. Since nothing can be taken beyond this life, it follows one should selfishly consume everything possible in the name of personal gratification while here on earth.

Ecclesiastes 5:15 states, "As he came forth of his mother's womb, naked shall he return to go as he came, and shall take nothing of his labour, which he may carry away in his hand."

Solomon's conclusion, however, is distinctly different from today's popularized philosophy. Solomon eventually realized his pursuits were foolishness. All of his attempts to find meaning in life without God were "empty vanity." These can never satisfy man's longing for purpose. Quite the contrary, such pursuits lead to loneliness, fear, isolation, selfishness, and ultimately desperation. As Solomon concludes, they become a "sore evil" (Ecclesiastes 5:16).

Bible Byte: Solomon, regarded as the Bible's wisest man, tried many of the world's trappings. But scripture offers his experience as a lesson from which we may learn to avoid his folly, not as a license to repeat his mistakes. Many of his points taken out of context miss the true inspired message God affords through Solomon's example.

Chapter 12 records Solomon's final considerations: "Let us hear the conclusion of the whole matter: Fear God, and keep his commandments: for this is the whole duty of man. For God shall bring every work into judgment, with every secret thing, whether it be good, or whether it be evil" (Ecclesiastes 12:13–14).

No, you can't take it with you. We can't take anything from this life. But, with God in your heart, you won't need anything else. Take hold of Solomon's lesson and take it with you to heaven.

Days Are Numbered

Psalm 90:12

Today's Phrase: As years fly by, my definition for old age is changing. Truthfully, I'm beyond several of my earlier bogies; but as the years continually drift by, my "old age" target will probably always remain just slightly beyond my reach. (My mental reach, at least.)

It's true; what sounded old when my father passed away is incredibly young today. And while in younger years I may have eagerly counted down the days until I got out of high school, college, or the military, I'm simply not as eager today to place those tick marks on the calendar.

Does this sound familiar? Most everyone eventually comes to the realization that our "days are numbered." Of course, I had heard that phrase as a child too, usually relating to some mischief I'd come to later regret. While my brother wasn't a snitch, I often recall his warning: "Your days are numbered if Dad finds out!"

Psalm 90 is the thought-provoking origin for this popular expression. And while also a warning, it illustrates a brighter promise than my brother's message.

Biblical Background: Titled "A Prayer of Moses the man of God," this Psalm is beautifully written. Only seventeen verses long, it poetically describes the misery and fear of separation from God brought about by the "iniquities" and "secret sins" of men. It is also a call to repentance: "Return, ye children of men" (verse 3). The writer fearfully acknowledges

God's everlasting majesty and pleads for mercy to allow return unto joy and gladness in fellowship with Him.

The timeless nature of God is revealed in verse 4: "For a thousand years in thy sight are but as yesterday when it is past" And verse 12 states, "So teach us to number our days, that we may apply our hearts unto wisdom." The Psalm concludes with this plea: "Let the beauty of the LORD be upon us" (Psalm 90:17).

Bible Byte: Yes, our days are, in fact, numbered. As a child, when my brother sounded that warning, I knew the day of reckoning had arrived. Psalm 90 also contains a warning, but the emphasis is on hope, not fear. Moses's prayer alludes to a day of reckoning. But he also teaches us to count on God, not on ourselves. I reckon that's the best way to "let the beauty of the LORD our God be upon us."

Do as I Say, Not as I Do

Matthew 23:3

Today's Phrase: My father was a heavy smoker, and I'll always picture him with a cigarette. I recall the brand he smoked, how he would hold it in his hand, and even how he lit the match. In spite of his long-standing, self-avowed "nasty habit," Dad always discouraged us kids from smoking. "But *you* smoke, Dad," we'd say, confronting his bad example. Predictably, he dismissed our challenge tersely: "Do as I say, not as I do!"

We discussed a *lot* of things that way in my house. Dad ruled with a strong hand; clearly, there were different rules for him than for us. Believe it or not, authority figures have been using this tactic for almost two thousand years. Jesus's words in Matthew 23:3 are the fascinating origin for this popular parental ploy.

Biblical Background: Jesus clearly taught respect for authority. He acknowledged church leaders of His day and recognized their position over the people. When addressing a crowd, Jesus counseled to "observe and do" what the Pharisees bid them to do. "But do not ye after their works: for they say, and do not" (Matthew 23:3). What did they say? The Pharisees preached strict compliance with a multitude of religious laws and ordinances, but they cleverly complied only outwardly. In chapter 23, Christ calls them "hypocrites," "blind guides," "fools," and "vipers." He denounces their self-serving, self-righteous works.

Bible Byte: Christ said, in effect, "Do what they say, not what they do." But He was not condoning their works. On the contrary, their abuse of authority was just as unacceptable to Jesus as it is to any teen today. Interestingly, there have been studies in the field of education that suggest children remember only ten percent of what they hear and ninety percent of what they see. Clearly, there is no better teacher than a good example. That's a sobering thought as now I'm sometimes tempted to use my dad's old line with my kids.

Clearly, the greater challenge is to consider Jesus and follow *His* example.

Drop in the Bucket

Isaiah 40:15

Today's Phrase: Have you browsed a bookstore recently? Shelves are packed with self-help books. Modern psychology admits to an epidemic absence of self-esteem, and that deep pit has been filled by an ocean of remedies promoting everything from self-hypnosis to the "power" of positive thinking. Unfortunately, many people today judge themselves insignificant by society's standards. They see themselves as an insignificant drop in society's bucket, hardly noticed and inconsequential. Awash in a flood of humanist ideas, it's imperative we examine the biblical standard. It, too, has something to say about the familiar figure of speech "a drop in the bucket."

Biblical Background: Isaiah compares man's significance to the majesty of God by posing a series of questions beginning in verse 12: "Who hath measured the waters [oceans] in the hollow of his hand, and meted out [or measured] heaven with the span [a distance of about 9 inches]?" Verse 13 adds, "Who hath directed the Spirit of the LORD, or being his counsellor hath taught him?" As important as man self-centeredly believes he is, Isaiah provides a godly perspective: "Behold, the nations are as a drop of a bucket, and are counted as the small dust of the balance" (Isaiah 40:15). This passage affirms man is, in fact, insignificant. But it is compared with *God, not one another.* Satan has set a subtle snare. On the one hand, his influence has so permeated society that our concept of self-worth is corrupted. The problem is worsened by the world's fantasy standards. Consider the entertainment media, for example. Glitter and glamour distort reality to an unrealistic standard, inviting both comparison and disappointment. We face inevitable shortfall by this yardstick. A negative self-image results, and we judge ourselves "an inconsequential drop in society's bucket." On the other hand, for those with poor self-esteem, Satan spins an intricate web of humanist philosophy that entangles souls in the illusion they can find peace apart from God. Satan is playing both ends against the middle, and we're in the squeeze.

Bible Byte: Humanist teachings suggest that man directs his own destiny, reigns supreme, and is, in fact, a type of God. Isaiah provides a different prescription. Verse 26 states, "Lift up your eyes on high" and verse 29 declares, "He giveth power to the faint." In other words, by the very admission of our weakness, God will compassionately strengthen us. We need only look to Him, not ourselves. Only God's approval matters. Society's standards are a drop in the bucket.

Down to Brass Tacks

Exodus 26:11
Exodus 36:18

Today's Phrase: "Getting down to brass tacks" implies detail, nitty-gritty elements of detail. Researching the origin for this phrase led to some interesting possibilities. One source suggested the phrase originated from a technique used by early merchants to measure fabric. Brass tacks, driven into the countertop, were spaced exactly one yard apart to eliminate guesswork from measurements. If a clerk would hold a bolt of cloth up to approximate, a customer might demand, "Hey! Let's quit guessing and get down to brass tacks." The Old Testament book of Exodus, however, suggests quite a different origin.

Biblical Background: Exodus 25 begins with God's direction to the Hebrew nation: "Let them make me a sanctuary; that I may dwell among them. According to all that I shew thee, after the pattern of the tabernacle, and the pattern of all the instruments thereof, even so shall ye make it" (Exodus 25:8–9). What follows is an incredible oration of elaborate, if not excruciating, detail. Reading through the instructions is almost as laborious as the details themselves. Every conceivable item is spelled out: size, shape, material, and construction details. It's an elaborate blueprint of painstaking description.

Exodus 26:11 mentions "taches of brass," which were small brass clasps used to secure the veil or curtain. A steady stream of detail meanders throughout subsequent chapters until chapter 36, verse 18, again mentions these seemingly insignificant "taches of brass." Though small, these clasps were critical to hold the veil together as a unit.

Reading through the Exodus details, it becomes clear that over time we have appropriated the term "brass tacks" as a synonym for essential detail. Often the phrase is used in similar context as Exodus: "Let's get down to those small elements of detail that hold things together."

Bible Byte: God clearly had specific plans for the tabernacle. Although it's not quite so clear what His specific plans are for our lives, just as He sought a dwelling place with the Jewish people, He seeks that same dwelling place within us.

The veil of the temple was torn in two at Christ's crucifixion, symbolically removing the separation of man from God. He no longer resides in the temple; he resides in the hearts of men who invite Him in. Now there's a detail you won't want to overlook. And don't overlook an opportunity to share *that* essential fact the next time you hear someone say, "Let's get down to brass tacks."

Down to the Last Iota
Fits to a T

Matthew 5:18

Today's Phrase: A common phrase describing the "persnicketiness" of a perfectionist might sound something like, "Wow, they make sure everything is perfect, right down to the last iota." Or, when clothing is flattering and fits comfortably, we might say, "That fits you to a *T*." These are common phrases, but quite strange when you think about them. What is an "iota"? How has that come to symbolize perfection? Or how does something "fit to a *T*"? What or how does a *T* fit?

While I found no coo berating references, let's examine a possible biblical origin for these phrases.

Biblical Background: Matthew 5:17–18 states, "Think not that I am come to destroy the law, or the prophets: I am not come to destroy, but to fulfil. For verily I say unto you, Till heaven and earth pass, one jot or one tittle shall in no wise pass from the law, till all be fulfilled."

What does that prove? I admit it's not terribly clear. But the ancient Greek alphabet holds a clue. As you probably know, the New Testament was written in Greek. The smallest letter in the Greek alphabet was the letter "iota." Sometime during the eighteenth century, according to scholars, the Greek letter *i* was interchanged with *j*; hence, "iota" developed the shortened form "jot." As a result, "jot," translated in this passage from Christ's Sermon on the Mount, signifies small detail, insignificant detail, right down to the smallest letter, the last iota.

Similarly, the word "tittle" refers to the intricate brush marks made by ancient scribes when transcribing scriptures. These marks, sometimes called "horns," though seemingly insignificant, were signs of painstaking detail, similar to today's expression "dot all the i's and cross all the t's." Hence, "tittle" in this biblical passage symbolizes exacting detail, down to the finest brush mark or "cross" of a *t*. And Christ's words said, in effect, the finest details of the law had been fulfilled in His coming. But the Jewish leaders rejected Him.

Bible Byte: Today, when we use the phrases "down to the last iota" or "fit to a *T*," we imply perfection, intricate detail, and precision. Christ implied a similar meaning in His ancient mountainside sermon.

The scribes and Pharisees, though they taught the law, could not keep it. But Jesus *lived* a perfect life in fulfillment of the law. He was the only man able to master the law in both letter and spirit. While Jewish leaders were angry with Christ for His teachings, He was actually fulfilling both the law (through perfect love) and all that the prophets had foretold (through His sacrificial life). Christ's life perfectly fulfilled both Mosaic law and prophecy, but the Jewish leaders of that day failed to see it.

Hopefully, today you can recognize Christ's life as the representation of perfect man and see His death and resurrection as man's salvation. Go ahead, examine the Bible up close. You'll find it accurate "down to the last iota." Hopefully, you'll recognize God's purpose for your life "fits you to a *T*."

Don't Look Back

Genesis 19:17

Today's Phrase: It is often said that hindsight is twenty-twenty. Sure, it is easy to reflect on past choices and decisions, or paths trodden to see that we should have done things differently. But, while it's good to learn from the past, generally speaking, most counselors agree that, once you choose a direction, you should forge ahead. "Don't look back" is a motto for perseverance and progress. Interestingly, the Bible had something to say about this as well.

Biblical Background: Perhaps no ancient cities were more notoriously perverse than Sodom and Gomorrah. They are a stereotypical image of evil yet today. Open homosexuality was a rampant perversion practiced there. In fact, we get our word "sodomy" from the unnatural lusts prevalent within these cities. The story of one man's escape from this wickedness provides the background for the phrase "don't look back."

In Genesis 18:20, God condemned the sin within Sodom and Gomorrah, promising destruction for all inhabitants. Abraham pleaded with the Lord to spare His wrath for the sake of the righteous, and God agreed to spare these cities if but ten righteous could be found within their gates.

But only Lot and his family were found. God sent two angels who abided with Lot, his wife, and his two daughters. The depth of perversion among the people is revealed in verse 5 as the men of the city cried unto Lot to turn over these strangers, that the crowd may "know them." There is no mistaking the sexual perversion implied. The lust-filled crowd pressed toward the door to Lot's home, attempting to break it down to overtake the two strangers. The angels smote them blind and then commanded that Lot flee with his family to avoid the cities' destruction. "Escape for thy life; look not behind thee … lest thou be consumed" (Genesis 19:17).

As the story continues, we learn that, while the Lord mercifully permitted their escape, Lot's wife had difficulty with faithful obedience. Lot's wife looked back just as the cities were being destroyed. Verse 26 states, "But his wife looked back from behind him, and she became a pillar of salt."

Bible Byte: Why the instruction to "look not behind thee"? Perhaps Philippians provides the best clue: "This one thing I do, forgetting those things which are behind … I press toward the mark for the prize of the high calling of God in Christ Jesus" (Philippians 3:13–14).

When we focus on the failures of our past, we may miss the God-given opportunities for success in our future. And just as God calls us forth to depart the certain destruction of a sinful life, we must avoid the temptation to look back, choosing instead to faithfully look forward. Once you've come to Christ, keep your eyes on Him. "Don't look back." There's nothing worth going back for.

Double-Edged Sword
Two-Edged Sword

Revelation 1:16
Hebrews 4:12

Today's Phrase: When faced with a particularly tough decision, I sometimes make a list of pros and cons. It can help to weigh the consequences of my choice and also takes a bit of the emotion out of a tough decision. Once in a while, there's an option that looks good on the surface and maybe tempting to try on impulse. When I examine the pros and cons, however, it becomes a little clearer that often these tempting choices are "double-edged swords."

The implication of this expression is "Be careful; use good judgment. There are some consequences to consider." In the Bible, the "double-edged sword" also deals with judgment. But as you might expect, it's slightly different.

Biblical Background: Revelation is a remarkable book. It's difficult to understand, certainly, but chapter 1, verse 3, states there is blessing to be received simply by reading and hearing the words of this prophecy. The book is titled "The Revelation of St. John the Divine" in the King James Bible, yet chapter 1 immediately sets us straight that it is the revelation of Christ given unto John: "The Revelation of Jesus Christ, which God gave unto him, to shew unto his servants things which must shortly come to pass; and he sent and signified it by his angel unto his servant

John: Who bare record of the word of God, and of the testimony of Jesus Christ, and of all things that he saw" (Revelation 1:1–2).

One of the visions John saw was the glorified Christ. It must have been overwhelming as John admits in verse 17: "And when I saw him, I fell at his feet as dead." The description John records in verses 12–16 is a frightening picture. Verse 16 contains the reference to the double-edged sword: "And he had in his right hand seven stars: and out of his mouth went a sharp twoedged sword: and his countenance was as the sun shineth in his strength."

What does the two-edged sword symbolize? Hebrews 4:12 holds the key: "For the word of God is quick, and powerful, and sharper than any twoedged sword, piercing even to the dividing asunder of soul and spirit, and of the joints and marrow, and is a discerner of the thoughts and intents of the heart." In other words, the "twoedged sword" is the word of God.

John saw Christ, the glorified and resurrected Christ, and out of His mouth came words of judgment. Reading further in Revelation, we find that Christ, through John, delivers a word of judgment to the seven churches of history. I'll not attempt to interpret those judgments; but clearly, God judges by His word.

Bible Byte: "Be careful; use good judgment; proceed with caution"; that's the modern implication of the phrase "double-edged" or "two-edged sword." There are consequences of our choices, and it's wise to be careful.

The biblical context for this phrase is also one of judgment—God's judgment. He, too, has a list of pros and cons. The pros are those *for* Christ; the cons are those set against Him. Considering the fearful and awesome figure John depicts of the glorified Christ, shouldn't you choose which side you're on?

Dead to the World

Colossians 3:5

Today's Phrase: I've probably never worked harder, certainly no *longer* hours, than while at sea during my navy years. There wasn't much opportunity for sleep when our ship pulled out of home port. Operating hundreds of miles from shore, that two-hundred-foot vessel placed heavy demands on our small crew. Ten-hour workdays with eight additional hours of watch duty were the norm. When the opportunity for bunk time arrived, precious sleep came quickly. More than once I recall the security patrol trying to rouse me from my "rack" to relieve the midnight watch. As the fog in my head cleared, I'd hear his familiar words: "Dead to the world, huh, sir?"

Yes, I was "dead to the world," fast asleep. But this phrase can also imply being oblivious to what's going on, even when wide-awake. For example, someone deep in thought or lost in a daydream might be termed "dead to the world." Paul's letter to the Colossians provides a convincing argument for the biblical roots of this phrase.

Biblical Background: Colossians 3 presents Paul's exhortation to believers at Colossae. Paul reminds these new Christians that they are risen with Christ; therefore, their affections and desires should be set on those things "above," heavenly desires, not worldly desires.

"For ye are dead, and your life is hid with Christ in God" (Colossians 3:3). "Mortify therefore your members which are upon the earth"

(Colossians 3:5). Mortify means to subdue or deaden. Paul's message suggests these new believers are dead, yet alive—dead to the world, yet alive in Christ.

Bible Byte: Through time, we have appropriated this expression in a fascinating way. Just as Paul encouraged believers to separate themselves from the world, we use "dead to the world" to describe the separation provided by sleep or by deep and consuming thoughts. Deeply satisfying and peaceful sleep or completely absorbing daydreams create the same effect, a separation from the realities of the world. And to be separated from the evils of this world brings the same satisfying peace implied by today's expression.

Christ said in Matthew 11:28, "Come unto me, all ye that labour and are heavy laden, and I will give you rest." His peace "passes all understanding" (Philippians 4:7).

In other words, there's nothing like it. Come and rest in Christ; become completely absorbed in Him. He will give you rest. And, even the world agrees, there's nothing like a good night's rest.

Don't Wear Out Your Welcome

Proverbs 25:17

Today's Phrase: My wife is a terrific visitor. I'm not. When we travel out of state to visit friends, I'm always voting for a hotel. She enjoys staying as houseguests. I give in reluctantly, but always with the understanding that we must be careful to ensure we don't wear out our welcome. And, (I hope our friends would agree), we generally let that sentiment be our guide.

Though the Bible encourages hospitality, it also contains a caveat on overstaying one's welcome. Solomon's book of Proverbs is the original recorded use of this wise and ageless sentiment.

Biblical Background: "Withdraw thy foot from thy neighbour's house; lest he be weary of thee, and so hate thee" (Proverbs 25:17). The English Revised version says, "Let thy foot be seldom in thy neighbour's house; lest he be weary of thee, and hate thee".

In either case, the admonition is clear: do not become a burden. The Bible teaches there was no one as wise as Solomon; and in my opinion, this expression confirms it.

Bible Byte: 1 Peter 4:9 states, "Use hospitality one to another without grudging." But this is no contradiction. Give hospitality freely; take hospitality in moderation. The emphasis is clear. If we're to be "out of balance," we're to err on the side of *giving*, not taking.

One day, if you depart this life as a believer in Jesus Christ, God will welcome you to his heavenly mansion. And there you'll never have to worry about wearing out your welcome. His house will be your house. There's plenty of room, but you'll still need to make a reservation. Call upon Him today; His line is open.

An Eye for an Eye

Exodus 21:24
Deuteronomy 19:21

Today's Phrase: Digging into etymology reveals surprising scriptural roots for many popular expressions. There are several colloquial sayings, however, which are of obvious biblical origin. "Doubting Thomas," "Good Samaritan," and others come to mind. "An eye for an eye" is also commonly associated with the Bible, and I expected many academic sources would confirm this. To my surprise, no references suggested its biblical roots. Instead, the earliest mention relates to an ancient Pyrenees battle in 778 AD. However, two ancient Old Testament passages contain the phrase and significantly predate that event.

Biblical Background: Exodus 21:24 and Deuteronomy 19:21 relate to ancient Jewish laws of restitution. Deuteronomy prescribes the punishment for making false accusations. False witness was regarded seriously in Mosaic law, and leniency was sparse. Judgment mirrored the offense requiring "life shall go for life, eye for eye, tooth for tooth" (Deuteronomy 19:21).

The law in Exodus also deals with a relevant subject of our day. Chapter 21, verses 18–27, prescribe the punishment for inflicting personal injury to others. Especially intriguing is the law which dealt with harm to "a woman with child, so that her fruit depart from her" (Exodus 21:22). If an expectant mother's child was killed, Old Testament law prescribed the judgment "eye for eye, tooth for tooth, hand for hand" (Exodus 21:24).

Bible Byte: The restitution dictated by Jewish law seems severe, but the reason for the law's severity is given in Deuteronomy: "So shalt thou put the evil away from among you. And those which remain shall hear, and fear, and shall henceforth commit no more any such evil among you" (Deuteronomy 19:19–20).

Sadly, generations later, those evils are yet with us. Modern society still deals with the tragedies inflicted by the evils of false accusation and murder. The courts overflow with lawsuits for slander and libel. And perhaps no evil plagues the nation more than the innocent slaughter of millions of babies through abortion.

In ancient Israel, Jewish law was severe, yet the law did not save the nation or its people. Nor can our laws today. Only Christ, who fulfilled the law, can save men and nations. Without the covering of Christ's blood, man will be judged severely. And God's day of judgment is coming. You will not be able to make restitution. Only through Christ has the sin debt been paid, paid in full. He gave His life for your life; why not give to Him what He already paid for?

Earmarked

Exodus 21:5–6
Deuteronomy 15:16–17

Today's Phrase: Something old, something new, something borrowed, something blue—any bride could identify this old rhyme as a description of articles to be worn on her wedding day. The origin for the superstition is unknown; but tradition suggests, when these articles are worn on the wedding day, good luck and happiness are assured.

My wife wore something from each category. While neither of us would credit a happy marriage to its effect, the tradition is both fun and charming. The old necklace worn by my wife belonged to her great-aunt. She still has it safely tucked away, "earmarked" for a future special day in our own daughters' lives.

"Earmarked" seems a rather odd and curious expression. It symbolizes special significance or stature. An individual may be "earmarked" for a special position, or an heirloom for a special occasion. The term is rooted in both Exodus and Deuteronomy.

Biblical Background: Exodus 21 lays down God's directives for master–servant relationships. In Hebrew culture, law made it clear that the Israelites could not permanently enslave one of their own in servitude: "If thou buy an Hebrew servant, six years he shall serve: and in the seventh he shall go out free for nothing" (Exodus 21:2).

A servant could, however, choose to stay on with his master, if desired:

"And if the servant shall plainly say, I love my master, my wife, and my children; I will not go out free: Then his master shall bring him unto the judges; he shall also bring him to the door, or unto the door post; and his master shall bore his ear through with an aul; and he shall serve him for ever" (Exodus 21:5–6). In other words, the servant would be "earmarked" to distinguish his service. No longer a slave, such an individual was serving by choice, by free will, and his mark signified his choice forever.

Bible Byte: "But he that is greatest among you shall be your servant" (Matthew 23:11). Christ calls us to serve others, not in anticipation of reward but rather as a free will choice. Let your life truly be "earmarked" for something special—service unto others. That's the mark of a believer. Make a choice for Christ, forever.

Eat 'Til It Comes Out of Your Nose

Numbers 4:11

Today's Phrase: As a child growing up, my least favorite meal was goulash. It seemed like we had it once a week, in spite of my protests. Most traumatic, however, was the generosity of my mother's portions. I can remember platefuls that must have weighed *two pounds*.

Naturally, I complained, played with my food, faked being sick … anything to get out of eating that stuff. "But Mom," I'd whine, "we *always* have goulash … I'm sick of goulash … give me something else … *anything* else!"

And just as predictably, Mom was unyielding, knowing, as mothers do, that this nutritious meal would satisfy my needs, even if not my palate. On more than one occasion she'd warn, "You're going to eat that goulash *until it comes out of your nose*!" Who would imagine that the Old Testament book of Numbers is the origin for that oft-spoken warning from Mom?

Biblical Background: The story unfolds in Numbers 11. The Israelite people were wandering in the wilderness, led by Moses, seeking the promised land. For food, they ate heavenly manna, a type of cake flour mixture that God miraculously provided throughout their journey. We're told it had the taste of fresh oil, but my impression is it must have resembled the bland doughy taste of a burrito shell. After several weeks of manna, the people murmured against Moses and God, longing for the good old days when they ate cucumbers, leeks, onion, garlic, and melons in Egypt.

Moses appealed to the Lord, "Whence should I have flesh to give unto this people? for they weep unto me, saying, Give us flesh, that we may eat" (Numbers 11:13). In other words, they were whining for something different. Like so often happens, they wished for what could be, versus being thankful for what they already had.

The Lord told Moses he had heard their weeping and commanded that Moses instruct the people to sanctify themselves, "For on the morrow they will eat flesh." " (Numbers 11:18). But two verses reflect the Lord's displeasure with their ingratitude: "Ye shall not eat one day, nor two days, nor five days, neither ten days, nor twenty days; But even a whole month, until it come out at your nostrils, and it be loathsome unto you" (Numbers 11:19–20).

Bible Byte: Sounds like an old mom, doesn't it? And it provides a rich lesson from the pages of scripture to teach us about gratitude. Being thankful for what we have pleases God. Whining for what we don't have is ungrateful. And even today, when I eat goulash, I think of Mom. I hope that pleases her.

The Error of His Ways

James 5:20

Today's Phrase: I moved around a lot as a child. As a result, I attended six different grade schools and two high schools. Some pained memories include a frequent and familiar scene as the class bully tried on the "new kid." If I dared to risk a little self-defense, the teasing could easily escalate into a very real threat of physical harm. I remember one particularly threatening thug who vowed to teach me "the error of my ways."

Of course, that scenario describes but one modern usage of the expression "the error of his ways," but it's one perhaps many can relate to. The biblical background of this phrase, found in the book of James, is quite different, however.

Biblical Background: James states, "If any of you do err from the truth, and one convert him; Let him know, that he which converteth the sinner from the error of his way shall save a soul from death, and shall hide a multitude of sins" (James 5:19–20).

Bible Byte: God will never "bully" man into submission. He lovingly created us with a free will. We can choose the ways of men or the ways of God. Of course, our natural way of sin separates us from the Father. God's way is through the Lord Jesus Christ. In John's gospel Jesus says "I am the way, the truth, and the life: no man cometh unto the Father, but by me" (John 14:6).

Through Jesus, we have an advocate with the Father. And, His shed blood covers a "multitude of sins." With any other choice, man foolishly risks "self-defense" and will ultimately regret the error of his way.

Feet of Clay

Daniel 2:33

Today's Phrase: "Feet of clay" is an odd expression synonymous with a fatal human flaw. The weakness is so serious or severe that it typically leads to failure or a man's undoing. In the business realm, it might be casually expressed, "We thought Smith was the man for the job, but unfortunately, he had feet of clay." This unique expression is derived from an equally unique biblical prophecy from the Old Testament book of Daniel. Daniel 2 relates the story.

Biblical Background: Nebuchadnezzar's kingdom was great. But, as he contemplated the future, pondering, "Where will it lead?" or "What will it come to?", he was troubled, suffering many sleepless nights. God, who knew the future, answered the king's questions in a dream.

Unfortunately, King Nebuchadnezzar didn't understand God's answer. He called in his wise men for an interpretation but would not tell them what the dream was. Perhaps he forgot it as he states in verse 5, "The thing is gone from me," or perhaps his skepticism is revealed. If his wise astrologers and magicians could reveal both the dream and its meaning, then certainly their interpretation could be believed. If not, perhaps their input was suspect. Of course, his wise men appealed, saying his demands were unreasonable. "None other that can shew it before the king, except the gods" (Daniel 2:11). Because his sage advisors were unyielding, the king furiously ordered their execution.

The stage is now remarkably set for Daniel, a Jewish captive, to be used by God. The captain of the guard told Daniel what happened, and Daniel seized the opportunity. He asked for an audience with the king to show him both the dream and its interpretation. Such brash confidence seems presumptuous, but verse 18 reveals that Daniel relied not on himself but upon God. In other words, he prayed that God would reveal it unto him.

God answered his plea. That night, the same vision and interpretation were given to Daniel and Daniel prayerfully thanked God for his provision.

Daniel eventually stood before the king and related both the dream and its meaning. King Nebuchadnezzar was amazed as Daniel described in perfect detail the strange and terrible image he had envisioned: a head of gold, breast and arms of silver, belly and thighs of brass, legs of iron, and feet of iron mixed with clay. Daniel continued to describe the destruction of the image, saying a stone "cut out without hands" would strike the image upon the feet of iron and clay, breaking them into pieces, while the other metals would be ground into powder and carried away by the wind.

The interpretations of King Nebuchadnezzar's dream have been often applied to the coming end-times. Many renowned expositors have taught the prophecy as it relates to our current world. While fascinating, that's beyond both my purpose and, quite frankly, capability. But insight into today's popular usage of the expression "feet of clay" can be gained by examining Daniel's interpretation.

Daniel told King Nebuchadnezzar that the head of gold in the image symbolized his kingdom. As the king contemplated the future, God revealed that many kingdoms would arise after him that would be inferior, just as silver, brass, and iron are inferior to gold. Finally, the last kingdom was pictured as a mixture of iron and clay, partly strong and partly weak. Verse 44 states, "And in the days of these kings shall the God of heaven set up a kingdom, which shall never be destroyed … it shall break in pieces and consume all these kingdoms, and it shall stand for ever."

Bible Byte: Just as "feet of clay" is colloquially used today as a symbol of weakness, in Nebuchadnezzar's dream, it is the symbol for the final fatal flaw of man's earthly kingdoms. Through history, each attempt for world rule has failed. Man's efforts will never stand apart from God.

Many Bible prophecy teachers tell us we're living in the latter earthly kingdom of iron and clay, partly strong and partly weak. The stone in Nebuchadnezzar's dream, which symbolizes Christ, will soon come to smash man's earthly kingdom to pieces as judgment for our fatal flaw, the flaw of sin.

How about you? Where are you standing? If it's in the world's "clay," you need to get more solid footing. Try Christ; be a part of His kingdom. Stand firm on the solid rock, and you'll stand for eternity.

Fuel the Fire

Proverbs 26:20

Today's Phrase: "Did you hear about Jane (or Bob or Bill or Susan)?" Oh, how we love to gossip. It's an insidious and contagious infection. If one begins, several will jump into the conversation to "fuel the fire." Solomon's book of Proverbs is the biblical origin for today's colloquial expression.

Biblical Background: Proverbs states, "Where no wood is, there the fire goeth out: so where there is no talebearer, the strife ceaseth. As coals are to burning coals, and wood to fire; so is a contentious man to kindle strife" (Proverbs 26:20–21).

Bible Byte: So much is said in so few words. Gossip is the fuel of the talebearers' fire. Without the fuel, the strife stops. Don't be a flame-fanner. Put the fire out before it spreads. As Smokey says, "Only YOU Can Prevent Forest Fires!"

Fly in the Ointment

Ecclesiastes 10:1

Today's Phrase: In this world, where it seems everyone is after the fast buck, nothing evokes more skepticism than the promise of a good deal. We are conditioned, I presume, by society's motto "You never get something for nothing." The popular expression "fly in the ointment" is one often used to illustrate that skepticism. I've heard it frequently in the business world, usually as a warning to "proceed with caution; something isn't right in this deal." Solomon also wrote about a "fly in the ointment." His phrase is originally found in Ecclesiastes 10.

Biblical Background: Solomon presents an analogy that sheds some light on the common sentiment expressed by today's phrase. In part, it reads, "Dead flies cause the ointment of the apothecary to send forth a stinking savour" (Ecclesiastes 10:1).

An apothecary is another name for today's modern neighborhood pharmacist. Certainly, we don't hesitate to rely on his myriad prescriptions for relief, "ointments" to salve life's irritations. We willingly trust his training, judgment, and reputation. Once that reputation is tarnished, however, he's in trouble. And that's the Bible's conclusion as well.

Let's look further in verse 1 to complete Solomon's picture: "So doth a little folly him that is in reputation for wisdom and honor." In other words, just as a rotten prescription destroys trust in the pharmacist, foolishness weakens a good reputation. Actually, the biblical context states it so strongly as to suggest folly *putrefies* a good reputation, just like dead flies in the ointment!

Bible Byte: Today, we are a society that desperately wants to believe in the inherent goodness of man. However, too often people are disappointed by the greed, selfishness, and dishonesty of others. We've come by our skepticism justifiably. Sin has conditioned us to expect not "good deals" but "dead flies" in dealing with our fellow man. It appears that the world needs a new prescription, and Christ is the best pharmacist in the neighborhood.

Forbidden Fruit

Genesis 2:17
Genesis 3:3

Today's Phrase: Society has obviously appropriated the phrase "forbidden fruit" from the biblical garden story of Adam and Eve. In Eve's case, it literally was the fruit from a special tree in the midst of God's garden. Today, it can be symbolic for anything desired but forbidden. Genesis 2–3 contains the familiar passage.

Biblical Background: Following creation, God planted a garden in Eden. "And there he put the man whom he had formed" (Genesis 2:8). God instructed Adam to tend the garden, commanding that he could freely eat from every tree but one, "the tree of knowledge of good and evil."

Chapter 3 is the familiar story of Eve's temptation. Just as he does today, Satan challenged God's authority. "Yea, hath God said, Ye shall not eat of every tree of the garden?" (Genesis 3:1). In other words, "Is it really so?" Eve answered Satan, explaining that they could eat of the fruit of all trees but that fruit from the tree of knowledge of good and evil was prohibited. "God hath said, Ye shall not eat of it, neither shall ye touch it, lest ye die" (Genesis 3:3).

Satan's subtle deceit charmed Eve into eventually yielding to her desires, and she ate of the "forbidden fruit." She subsequently offers the fruit to Adam, and he, too, eats. Their act of disobedience brought separation from God and introduced sin into the world. The perfection of the Garden of Eden was spoiled by sin.

Bible Byte: The term "Adam's apple" originates from the legend of Adam's bite of the "forbidden fruit." The story goes that the "apple" was forever stuck in his throat and is obvious yet today as a noticeable lump. Intriguingly, this characteristic is more pronounced in men than women. Perhaps that's God's reminder. When we longingly gaze at forbidden fruit, he wants us to remember Satan's subtle deception. The devil is a master of deceit, beguiling many to challenge God's authority. Satan tempts us with desirable things—"forbidden fruit." But God wants us to consider the consequences of our desire. Don't swallow Satan's lies completely. They can choke you to death, and at the very least, they'll leave a "lump in your throat."

Give Credit Where Credit Is Due

Romans 13:7

Today's Phrase: Today's economy revolves around credit. Everywhere consumers turn, there's an open invitation to "charge it." No wonder credit cards are termed "revolving charge cards." But the phrase "Give credit where credit is due" is most often related to recognition, tribute, or honor, not to money. We'll come back to the financial side later. For now, let's look at Paul's epistle to the Romans. It is credited as the source for today's popular expression.

Biblical Background: In Romans 13:7 Paul states, "Render therefore to all their dues: tribute to whom tribute is due; custom to whom custom; fear to whom fear; honour to whom honour" (Romans 13:7). In context, tribute and honor are synonymous with credit. Paul's exhortation is to "give credit where credit is due."

Bible Byte: Now, let's look again at the financial aspects of the word *credit*. An interesting parallel emerges. Ironically, those who need credit least are those most likely to be approved to get it. That's because the commercial finance world employs an approval scheme known as the "4 Cs" of credit: Character, Capacity to repay, Collateral [or security], and Conditions of payment.

In spiritual terms, mankind is a "debtor" race. The payment for sin is due. And we can't meet the payment. Like someone in desperate financial straits, mankind is in desperate spiritual need. Unfortunately, mankind can't qualify to repay the debt. Man's *character* is sinful; man has no *capacity* for a sinless life; man lacks *security* in himself, offering nothing as *collateral*; and finally, man's *condition* is unrighteous. No lender in the world would approve that debt.

Thankfully, God is a benevolent creditor. He not only recognized man's spiritually bankrupt condition but also paid sin's debt through His Son. Man, of himself, couldn't qualify; but God's 4 Cs are different: Christ's Compassionate Consent at Calvary. Through Christ's willing sacrifice, sin's debt is erased. Man deserves not credit but blame. The sin debt is ours. But the account is paid in full. Ironically, we can take no credit for ourselves. God deserves the praise. Let's thankfully give credit where credit is due.

Going to the Dogs

Matthew 7:6

Today's Phrase: When we hear the expression "going to the dogs," we immediately recognize the implication. Anything of value given to those who don't appreciate it becomes neglected, cheapened, or destroyed. A neighborhood "gone to the dogs" conjures images of peeling paint, splintered wood, and busted glass, homes that lack the basic care and attention required to preserve or protect them. This expression is derived from Christ's warning in Matthew 7:6.

Biblical Background: "Give not that which is holy unto the dogs, neither cast ye your pearls before swine" (Matthew 7:6).

Bible Byte: Today we place great value on our possessions and our image. We would be outraged to discover a neighbor neglecting their home. Selfishly, our concern would be the negative effects of depreciated values in the community.

What about the value we place on God's gift? Do we jealously guard it in a similar way? In Matthew, heaven is likened unto "one pearl of great price" (Matthew 13:46), worth a total personal sacrifice to obtain. At times, it would appear we Christians are content to neglect and cheapen that possession with greater emphasis on our material pursuits. Are we the ungrateful "swine" of our day, trampling God's gift underfoot?

Perhaps American Christians have things too easy. I found it sobering to hear that persecuted Christians in Russia continually pray for Americans to escape the trappings of wealth. When something is received freely, we ascribe less value to it. We work hard for material comforts and equally hard to protect them. We need be mindful that, while given freely, God's gift to man was not cheap. Christ paid a high price with His life, and to possess Him is priceless. Our continual challenge is to take care of and protect our Christian heritage from "going to ungrateful dogs." Take care of it. It's the best investment you'll ever make.

Go the Extra Mile

Matthew 5:41

Today's Phrase: In the business world, good service sells. A look at this nation's aging "rust belt" confirms the shift from manufacturing to service-oriented industries. Business competitors strive to achieve a level of service distinction and promise to "go that extra mile." However, many don't live up to that promise. I've heard it said that the extra mile has no traffic jam, implying few give that extra effort. In light of the biblical context and origin for this phrase, that's a sobering thought.

Biblical Background: The Sermon on the Mount contains Christ's challenge: "And whosoever shall compel thee to go a mile, go with him twain" (Matthew 5:41).

Bible Byte: Unfortunately, today, there is a tendency to "promise to go the distance while only delivering the dash." Our heavenly "trainer" is actively recruiting endurance runners, not sprinters. "Go the extra mile." You'll find the finish line worth the strain.

Gut Feeling

Proverbs 23:7

Today's Phrase: Human instinct is a subject of considerable debate. Many biologists theorize that all human behavior is socially learned and not inherently natural or inborn. Interestingly, our popular expression "gut feeling" implies man does possess an instinctive or intuitive sense of judgment. Many top executives actually credit their corporate success to decisions they've made based not on research or facts but rather on strong "gut feelings." Proverbs 23:7 is the origin for this commonly expressed sentiment.

Biblical Background: Very early translations of scripture record Proverbs 23:7 with these words: "As a man feels in his bowels—so he is." The King James Version reads, "As [a man] thinketh in his heart, so is he."

Bible Byte: Long ago, the bowels were considered the emotional center of the human being. We get our words "visceral" and "viscera," meaning internal organs, from this belief. Over time, human's emotional center has migrated to the heart. We can only guess why this has occurred. Certainly, the heart is an internal organ; but perhaps some romantic found it more pleasing to express love "with all his heart" rather than "all his bowels." We may never know.

Regardless, the phrase "gut feeling" logically relates to the former idea of human's emotional center being deep within the physical being.

Perhaps we could debate the existence of human instinct forever. Do we or don't we possess a natural instinct? My "gut feeling" suggests our Creator could settle the matter once and for all. He can settle your questions too. Ask Him.

Give Up the Ghost

John 19:30
Acts 5:10
Job 14:10

Today's Phrase: The expression "give up the ghost" means to give in, to surrender, to yield. In business, for example, it might be said, "Well, I thought we had a good sales lead there, but I guess we better give up the ghost and try a new approach." In this popular usage, the "ghost," of course, is figurative. In biblical context, the "ghost" was quite literally a reference to the spirit of man.

Biblical Background: Several Bible passages contain the phrase "give up the ghost," from Job's discourse on the brevity of life, "But man dieth, and wasteth away: yea, man giveth up the ghost and where is he?" (Job 14:10) to John's gospel account of Christ's crucifixion, "He said, It is finished: and he bowed his head, and gave up the ghost" (John 19:30).

Bible Byte: What is the answer to Job's question? Where is man's departed spirit? Christ said, "In my Father's house are many mansions … I go to prepare a place for you" (John 14:2). Clearly, we have a choice, a mansion in heaven or a dungeon in hell. Eventually, each of us will bow our head in death and "give up the ghost." A surrender to God today is a victory with God for eternity. That's the best "sales lead" you'll ever get. You better cash in on it.

Grace Period

Romans 6:14

Today's Phrase: An old axiom states, "Allow two days for a one-day job, and it will take two days to complete." This adage reflects insightfully upon the natural human penchant to procrastinate. From schoolwork to home projects or business assignments, we're deadline oriented, waiting until the last possible moment to do what we have to do. Many deadlines are flexed to allow for the common practice of foot-dragging with what is known as a "grace period."

The term "grace period" implies there is actually some extra time or a "second chance." Even though a deadline exists, it's understood, even expected, that many will go beyond it. The Bible, of course, has much to say about grace. While the term "grace period" is not specifically found, it's clearly inferred in scripture. Those inferences are very likely the origin for today's familiar expression.

Biblical Background: Romans contains the phrase "For ye are not under the law, but under grace" (Romans 6:14). In other words, the law relates to an absolute, but grace mitigates that law. Similarly, a deadline is an "absolute," but a "grace period" mitigates that absolute finality.

Bible Byte: Christian evangelists speak often today about the day of grace. They preach diligently to the unconverted that a day is coming when Jesus will return to judge the world's sin. A judgment day, or "deadline," is approaching. But, sadly, many people prefer to procrastinate. Even though they may accept that a deadline exists, they put off the decision to yield today, anticipating a "second chance" will come tomorrow.

Unfortunately, and realistically, there is no promise of tomorrow. We live in this "grace period" today, and it will one day expire. Once the "second chance" is gone, good intentions won't matter. As another popular saying puts it, the road to hell is paved with good intentions." Don't wait until the last minute when God's deadline comes. There will be no second chance for eternal life with God. Doesn't that put a whole new meaning to the term deadline?

He Really Thinks He's Something

Galatians 6:3

Today's Phrase: We all know one, you know, a self-centered, egotistical big-shot type. They enter a room with a swagger, nose up in the air, wanting to be both noticed and revered. These types are intimidating, to be sure; but quite frankly, they are met more often with contempt or disgust than reverence.

"Humph! He really thinks he's something." We've probably all used this phrase at one time or another. The Bible's original usage is similar, but it is a much more insightful look into the character of man. We've derived our modern expression from Paul's epistle to the Galatians.

Biblical Background: Paul's counsel to the Galatian church includes this exhortation: "Brethren, if a man be overtaken in a fault, ye which are spiritual, restore such an one in the spirit of meekness; considering thyself, lest thou also be tempted" (Galatians 6:1).

In other words, we all have faults. Don't be so quick to condemn or judge. And don't be so eager to place yourself above another person. There is none without fault. Paul continues, "Bear ye one another's burdens, and so fulfill the law of Christ. For if a man think himself to be something, when he is nothing, he deceiveth himself" (Galatians 6:2–3).

Bible Byte: Think about someone who fits the "he really thinks he's something" mold. Now reflect on the spiritual context of the biblical expression. We use it today with contempt. "He really thinks he's something," we snarl. The unspoken sentiment that we usually feel, but keep to ourselves, is an inevitable judgment: "But I know he's really nothing."

Paul's letter reminds us we all can fall prey to self-pride. We all deceive ourselves at times. But rather than contempt and judgment, Paul suggests compassion and understanding: "Bear one another's burdens, and so fulfill the law of Christ." Now, to live to that standard really *would* be something. It's certainly something to think about.

Hold My Tongue/Hold Your Tongue

Job 6:24
Job 13:19
Amos 6:10
Habakkuk 1:13

Today's Phrase: A vivid picture from my childhood memory is our family mealtime at the kitchen table. On the wall, squarely above the dining table, hung my father's favorite plaque. The raised block letters crowded the small ceramic dish. "Oh Lord, help me to keep my big mouth shut!" Today, when I hear the familiar expressions "hold my tongue" or "hold your tongue," I think of Dad's laughter as he so often referred to that plaque. Little did I realize the Bible is the source for that admonition and actually contains considerable teachings on the plagues of an unruly tongue.

Biblical Background: Several Old Testament scriptures (Job, Amos, and Habakkuk) contain the expression "hold my tongue," or "hold thy tongue." But the New Testament book of James offers the most intriguing challenge and insight regarding the problems of an unruly tongue.

James states, "If any man offend not in word, the same is a perfect man, and able also to bridle the whole body" (James 3:2). He further explains that even a strong horse will obey the control from a bit in its mouth and a mighty ship is directed by a tiny rudder: "Even so the tongue is a little member, and boasteth great things ... But the tongue can no man tame; it is an unruly evil, full of deadly poison. Therewith bless we God … and therewith curse we men … Out of the same mouth proceedeth blessing and cursing. My brethren, these things ought not so to be" (James 3:5–10).

Bible Byte: As I reflect upon Dad's plaque, he was, in his own way, teaching us to "hold our tongues." The tongue has been called the most powerful muscle in the body. As Dad knew, most of us are all too eager to give it a healthy workout.

If You Play with Fire, You're Gonna Get Burned

Proverbs 6:27–28

Today's Phrase: Temptation is a funny thing. Like a powerful magnet, it attracts the human heart. There is no immunity and no cure. It's unavoidable. Everyone faces temptation every day. If we act on the temptation, trouble invariably follows. The phrase "if you play with fire, you're gonna get burned" reminds us that there are consequences to our actions. And, the more dangerous the behavior, the more damaging the consequence. In the book of Proverbs, the original usage of this phrase, deals with a very hot topic.

Biblical Background: Proverbs contains great practical wisdom, which is as applicable today as it was when written: "My son, keep thy father's commandment, and forsake not the law of thy mother: Bind them continually upon thine heart, and tie them about thy neck. When thou goest, it shall lead thee; when thou sleepest, it shall keep thee; and when thou awakest, it shall talk with thee" (Proverbs 6:20–22).

Simply said, this warning says, "Young man, listen to your parents." The advice is certainly contemporary. "To keep thee from the evil woman, from the flattery of the tongue of a strange woman. Lust not after her beauty in thine heart; neither let her take thee with her eyelids. Can a man take fire in his bosom, and his clothes not be burned? Can one go upon hot coals, and his feet not be burned" (Proverbs 6:24–25, 27–28).

Although ancient history, this is clearly not dated material. The wisdom is timeless, perhaps even more appropriate for today's sex-crazed society.

Bible Byte: Yes, temptation is common to man. And, there are many temptations beyond lust. Satan is a crafty foe, and he knows right where to attack our individual weaknesses. But, while no immunity from temptation exists, there is an escape. Paul's letter to the Corinthians explains, "There hath no temptation taken you but such as is common to man: but God is faithful, who will not suffer you to be tempted above that ye are able; but will with the temptation also make a way to escape, that ye may be able to bear it" (1 Corinthians 10:13).

There's always a way out. As appealing as the fires of temptation may be, the consequence of burning in hell is frightening. Lean on God. Allow Him to lead you out of temptation's fire and into the glow of His perfect love for you.

Ivory Tower/Ivory Palace

Song of Solomon 7:4
Psalm 45:8

Today's Phrase: Not unlike big government, large corporations are breeding grounds for complex, bureaucratic management systems. The order of the day is "rule by committee." Finding someone solely responsible for decisions is an improbable, if not impossible task. From such complex bureaucracies are spawned sarcastic referrals to corporate headquarters, such as "the ivory tower" or "the ivory palace." These sometimes contemptuous referrals at best symbolize the prestige and special status of top executives but more likely represent the insulation and separation subordinates feel from chief company officers.

The Old Testament books of Psalms and Song of Solomon both contain these phrases, but they have no trace of today's sarcasm.

Biblical Background: Song of Solomon is perhaps the most beautiful love song ever penned. Solomon refers to his beloved wife with admiring awe: "How beautiful are thy feet … thy thighs are like jewels … Thy navel is like a round goblet." He likens her belly to "an heap of wheat set about with lilies" and her breasts to "two twin roes, graceful and elegant." " Verses 4–6 continue his praise: "Thy neck is as a tower of ivory … How fair and how pleasant art thou, O love, for delights!"

Psalm 45, by contrast, is a portrayal of the eventual Messiah, Jesus Christ. The writer reverently describes the majesty and power of His reign. Verse 8 describes the finery of raiment and the fragrance of "myrrh, and aloes, and cassia, out of the ivory palaces." Both scriptures describe the beauty and majesty of their subject. Yet, in modern days, we commonly use these phrases sarcastically. Why the difference? Perhaps it's mere coincidence. Yet, again, perhaps it's but further evidence of how far we've strayed from both biblical context and biblical principal as well.

Bible Byte: Psalm 45:8 suggests the coming Messiah's garments would smell of myrrh, aloes, and cassia. All are a form of aromatic herb or resin used in ancient burial preparation. They are a symbol of Christ's prophetic suffering and burial. Certainly, Christ was contemptuously regarded by the ruling class of His time, mocked, sarcastically ridiculed, and ultimately crucified. Could it be that today's sarcastic referral to the "ivory palace" is a symbol of man's continued contempt for God? Could the sarcastic referral to the "ivory tower" reveal how far we've degenerated our view of the love between man and woman, from beauty and majesty to sleaze and pornography?

Perhaps it is coincidence. But the decay man has brought to this world suggests perhaps not. Many today treat both sexual love and God with contempt. It's time to turn that around. How? Make a decision for God. Check back in with the ultimate authority. There's room for you to be "promoted to headquarters."

In the Twinkling of an Eye

1 Corinthians 15:52

Today's Phrase: My father-in-law was a genuine wood craftsman. He was a perfectionist, to be sure, and very professional and meticulous. He had a well-equipped shop; and once in a while, I was privileged to work with him. He was as much a stickler with his equipment as he was with the craftsmanship of his products. And he had a very healthy respect for the danger of saws, jointers, planes, and the like.

"Watch it, Willy," he would warn, "you can lose a finger in the twinkling of an eye." Scripture originates the phrase "in the twinkling of an eye" and it, too, relates to an instant, one quick moment of time, when there will be no second chance.

Biblical Background: Chapter 15 of Paul's first letter to the Corinthians deals with the resurrection of Christ and the resurrection of believers at Christ's second coming. Paul's writings answer the skeptics and philosophers of his day as well as our own modern age:

"But if there be no resurrection of the dead, then is Christ not risen: And if Christ be not risen, then is our preaching vain, and your faith is also vain" (1 Corinthians 15:13–14).

"For if the dead rise not, then is not Christ raised: And if Christ be not raised, your faith is vain; ye are yet in your sins" (1 Corinthians 15:16–17).

Paul hits the issue head-on. If there is no resurrection, then Christ did not defeat death. And if Christ has no victory over death, our faith is worthless. Ultimately, Paul states, "If in this life only we have hope in Christ, we are of all men most miserable" (1 Corinthians 15:19). But Paul does not back down. He proclaims Christ is risen indeed and all who die will likewise be resurrected. Our physical bodies will be made alive again as glorified spiritual bodies: "In a moment, in the twinkling of an eye, at the last trump: for the trumpet shall sound, and the dead shall be raised incorruptible, and we shall be changed" (1 Corinthians 15:52).

Bible Byte: At any moment, in an instant as quick as the twinkling of an eye, Christ will return one day at the sound of a trumpet to call the dead back to life. These corrupt old bodies will be changed to glorified spiritual bodies. The victory of Christ's resurrection is proclaimed by Paul: "O death, where is thy sting? O grave, where is thy victory? The sting of death is sin; and the strength of sin is the law. But thanks be to God, which giveth us the victory through our Lord Jesus Christ" (1 Corinthians 15:55–57).

I heard once on the radio that General Electric scientists actually calculated the "twinkling of an eye" to be 0.11 seconds. Blink your eyes. Christ could come that quickly. Are you ready?

Just Reward

Hebrews 2:2

Today's Phrase: Many child psychologists caution parents today, "Don't teach your kids that life is fair." They believe, when parents try to ensure all is shared, divided, or rewarded equally among siblings, an unrealistic expectation for fairness in adult years is imparted. As these kids mature and assume their roles in a competitive world, cruel reality will quickly, perhaps harshly, reveal that life, in fact, isn't fair.

It may be an appropriate warning. Certainly, it's an interesting philosophical perspective; and I won't argue it has possible merit. But I must admit my personal tendencies attempt to achieve fairness with my children; and I doubt I'm alone. In fact, society's popular phrase "just reward" indicates most of us want and expect fairness from life.

If, for example, someone takes unfair advantage of another, we want to believe the wrongdoer will receive his "just reward." Likewise, when someone performs unselfishly, we, too, want that kindness rewarded justly. The Bible poses an interesting question regarding life's "just reward."

Biblical Background: Hebrews 2 states: "For if ... every transgression and disobedience received a just recompense of reward; How shall we escape, if we neglect so great salvation?" In other words, if sinful man "gets what he deserves," there is no escape but through the shed blood of Christ.

Bible Byte: For a moment, assume the psychologists are right: Let's not promote an erroneous perception among our youth. Life isn't fair. Let's tell them and teach them the way it is. Certainly, the "good guys" don't always win; and the "bad guys" don't always get what they deserve. But while life isn't fair, death becomes the great equalizer. All will face it; there is no escape.

Without Christ, man's "just reward" is hell. Without belief in His shed blood, we'll all get what we deserve. Surely, this lesson should be taught to our children. An erroneous perception on this issue affects not only the adult years of life but also all eternity. Let's study the Bible textbook and teach our children well. If we "get what we deserve," then death and hell await. But that need not be. Through God's grace, we have the promise of eternal life in heaven. Which reward will you receive?

Kiss of Death

Matthew 26:48

Today's Phrase: The trail from my college academic life is littered with poor grades in physics. It definitely was *not* my strong suit, and I suppose I never fully appreciated the purpose of mathematically dissecting the obvious. The only "law of physics" I can recall relates to something about every action creating an equal, opposite reaction. I do, however, recall in vivid, painful detail a specific reaction I had to a certain college professor.

After barely surviving first semester physics class with Professor Simpson, I was tragically reassigned to his class for the second term as well. As if physics wasn't bad enough, Simpson was the final "kiss of death," assuring my demise.

This common saying undoubtedly originates from the story of Judas's betrayal of Christ.

Biblical Background: The account of Judas's deceit is recorded in all four Gospels and is widely known, even among unbelievers. Many have exhaustively researched Judas's motivations for betrayal. Some theorize he wanted to force Christ to reveal His kingdom by orchestrating a confrontation with the Jewish political leaders. Others portray Judas as simply greedy, betraying our Lord for money.

Quite simply, I accept Christ's betrayal as foreordained; and Judas's personal motivation is truly insignificant. (Although his later return of the thirty pieces of silver suggest it was not for personal monetary gain.)

Matthew 26:47–49 relates how Judas delivered Christ into the hands of His captors: "Now he that betrayed him gave them a sign, saying, Whomsoever I shall kiss, that same is he: hold him fast" (Matthew 26:48).

Bible Byte: While Judas has been despised through the centuries for his treachery, we should remember it was not Judas's "kiss of death" that killed Christ. That simple act merely signaled the beginning of the process that led to Calvary. It merely foretold the beginning of the end. And yet, for believers Jesus's death is not defeat but victory. Christ's sacrifice was perfected in His willing submission to die at the hands of men. His glorious resurrection is a symbol of eternal hope for all believers.

In spite of the doom foretold by Judas's "kiss of death," Jesus eventually triumphed. We, too, can share in His victory. And, by the way, in spite of dreaded old Simpson, I managed to triumph over second semester physics as well.

Kiss His Feet

Luke 7:38

Today's Phrase: Arrogant people are a real turnoff. Some have their noses so high in the air they refuse to acknowledge those whom they consider to be the "little people." A phrase often disgustedly directed at this type of person typically goes like this: "He's such an egomaniac. He expects you to kiss his feet." Luke records the story that serves as the basis for today's expression.

Biblical Background: While Jesus offered a great deal of words condemning the Pharisees, He once accepted an invitation to the house of a Pharisee named Simon. He entered the house and sat down to dinner.

"And, behold, a woman in the city, which was a sinner, when she knew that Jesus sat at meat in the Pharisee's house, brought an alabaster box of ointment, And stood at his feet behind him weeping, and began to wash his feet with tears, and did wipe them with the hairs of her head, and kissed his feet, and anointed them with the ointment" (Luke 7:37–38).

Simon was repulsed at her act. He believed that Christ, if He were truly a prophet, would not have allowed a known sinner to touch and pollute Him. Christ, aware of Simon's contempt, answered him with a beautiful parable of two debtors: "There was a certain creditor which had two debtors: the one owed five hundred pence, and the other fifty.

And when they had nothing to pay, he frankly forgave them both. Tell me therefore, which of them will love him most? Simon answered and said, I suppose that he, to whom he forgave most. And he said unto him, Thou hast rightly judged" (Luke 7:40–43).

Christ then turned to the woman, and with His words of compassion, pointedly confronted Simon. "Seest thou this woman? I entered into thine house, thou gavest me no water for my feet: but she hath washed my feet with tears, and wiped them with the hairs of her head. Thou gavest me no kiss: but this woman since the time I came in hath not ceased to kiss my feet. My head with oil thou didst not anoint: but this woman hath anointed my feet with ointment. Wherefore I say unto thee, Her sins, which are many, are forgiven; for she loved much: but to whom little is forgiven, the same loveth little. And he said unto her, Thy sins are forgiven" (Luke 7:44–48).

Bible Byte: This grateful woman recognized her Lord. She knew His greatness. And she willingly "kissed his feet." Christ did not expect it, but he was clearly moved by her sacrificial act of love. The Pharisee, on the other hand, had his nose in the air. "If Christ were truly a prophet," he thought, "he would not permit this wretched sinner, this insignificant little woman, to touch Him." The Pharisee was a picture of arrogance, and the woman a picture of humility.

One day, we, too, will bow at Christ's feet. And, just as this woman in Luke, we will shed tears, tears of joy to hear Christ proclaim, "Arise, my child, thy sins are forgiven thee."

Love Is Blind

1 Peter 4:8

Today's Phrase: It's so easy to be critical and so hard to overlook the faults of others. (And naturally, it's so *tempting* to discuss them with other willing gossips.) Shame on me; I admit to engaging in some of these types of discussions. They usually go something like this: "I can't see how she puts up with his [blank]. Oh, well, you know what they say—love is blind." (The "blank" can be anything from snoring to snarling.)

Biblical Background: It shouldn't surprise us that the Bible first expressed love's ability to be a "great cover-up." 1 Peter 4:8 explains, "And above all things have fervent charity [love] among yourselves: for charity shall cover the multitude of sins."

This simple statement is remarkable; but there's one small word, which really impresses me. "Love shall cover *the* multitude of sins." The small article "the" is what's most amazing about this verse. If it were simply "*a* multitude of sins," then a finite limit would be implied, suggesting love could only go so far. Once a certain level of sin was exceeded, love couldn't cover it any longer. But the simple words "the multitude" imply the limitless ability love has to cover sin. No matter how great the multitude of sin is, love can cover it.

Bible Byte: In the gossip example above, our weak human reasoning can't comprehend a love that overlooks such apparent and obvious faults. But God, through His word, promises exactly that kind of love, a love that is unbounded, which has no limits. Wherever we are, whatever sins mar our lives, His love and forgiveness can cover it all: "Though your sins be as scarlet, they shall be white as snow" (Isaiah 1:18).

I'm reminded of a bumper sticker I've seen many times, saying "Christians Aren't Perfect—Just Forgiven!" It's comforting to know God sees believers through His Son, Jesus Christ. And Christ's love covers *the* multitude of sins. We're not worthy of fellowship with God; but through His Son, God's love is blind.

Laughter Is the Best Medicine

Proverbs 17:22

Today's Phrase: Modern medical science has repeatedly affirmed the "medicinal" value of laughter. Physicians frequently extol laughter's complement to the healing process and contrast its positive effects with the ravages caused by depression or a broken spirit. Though Solomon completed the book of Proverbs thousands of years ago, he penned a prescription that could be lifted right out of today's medical journals.

Biblical Background: He writes in chapter 17, "A merry heart doeth good like a medicine: but a broken spirit drieth the bones" (Proverbs 17:22).

Bible Byte: While Solomon's words have changed very little over centuries of time, this phrase has been embellished. Solomon acknowledged the "good" of laughter. Today, we term it the "best" medicine. Actually, the "best" medicine is provided by the Great Physician, Jesus Christ. He can mend the broken spirit and replace it with great joy.

Unfortunately, the unconverted soul harbors a misconception that Christians must be sober-faced, unhappy "killjoys". If it sounds like fun, it *can't* be Christian. Nonsense! Laughter and joy are a timeless prescription for physical and spiritual health. Let's share both our merry hearts and our Lord with every soul we meet. A broken spirit is no laughing matter.

A Little Birdie Told Me

Ecclesiastes 10:20

Today's Phrase: My wife and I recently celebrated our thirty-seventh wedding anniversary with a quiet, romantic dinner. We don't eat out often, and I was particularly looking forward to a quiet evening alone. We arrived at the restaurant late, around nine thirty, and I appreciated the absence of a crowd. We had just sat at our table when two couples we recognized strolled over to our table. I tried to be polite and patient, but I certainly did *not* want a "party." I quickly explained the special occasion, too quickly according to my wife, and it had the desired effect. We enjoyed our special dinner together, and alone. Later, following a fine meal, our waitress brought a large complimentary ice-cream, cake, whipped-cream, and strawberry dessert.

"Happy Anniversary!" she beamed. We were shocked.

"How did you know it was our anniversary?" my wife asked the waitress.

"Oh, *a little birdie told me*," came her reply. It didn't take long to realize our friends had arranged the surprise. My words came back to me, this time as a very pleasant surprise. But that's not always the case, as shown in the original passage from Ecclesiastes.

Biblical Background: "Curse not the king, no not in thy thought; and curse not the rich in thy bedchamber: for a bird of the air shall carry the voice, and that which hath wings shall tell the matter" (Ecclesiastes 10:20).

Bible Byte: An old poem entitled "The Laws of the Navy" comes to mind: "Beware what you say of your seniors; Be your words spoken softly and plain; Lest a bird of the air tell the matter; And so shall ye hear it again." Be careful; whatever you say might come back to you. It's a lesson for everyone. James states in the New Testament, "But the tongue can no man tame; it is an unruly evil, full of deadly poison" (James 3:8).

The temptation to gossip is strong. No one is immune. But, when everything you say can be spread by a "little birdie," it makes choosing your words very important. As David writes in Psalm 51:15, "O Lord, open thou my lips; and my mouth shall shew forth thy praise." Now these are words you'd be happy to hear repeated by any "little birdie."

A Leopard Doesn't Change Its Spots

Jeremiah 13:23

Today's Phrase: "If it acts and sounds like a duck, it probably *is* a duck." This humorous quote appears to be the modern slang equivalent of the ancient, yet still popular, saying "a leopard doesn't change its spots." Each expression can serve a dual role, as the caveat "beware" or as the after-the-fact affirmation "I told you so." Both colloquialisms express a time-tested truth. Character is internal not external. In other words, don't be fooled by an outward display; look deeper for hidden signs of true character. Jeremiah presents this premise prophetically in chapter 13 of the Old Testament book bearing his name.

Biblical Background: The nation of Israel rejected God, thereby reaping prophetic destruction. Their pride, idolatry, and iniquity incited God's jealousy and wrath. God foretells their inescapable punishment through the prophet Jeremiah with a warning, which effectively says: "Don't doubt in your heart that your sin merits destruction. You cannot hide it or cover it up" (Jeremiah 13:22). God's perception of true, internal character is perfect. He is not fooled by man's outward portrayals of righteousness.

"Can the Ethiopian change his skin, or the leopard his spots? then may ye also do good, that are accustomed to do evil" (Jeremiah 13:23).

In other words, man's outward attempts to mask true character are transparent to God. Just as the Ethiopian remains an Ethiopian despite the color of his skin or a leopard is still a leopard in spite of its outward coat, man's true nature is internally, not externally, determined.

Bible Byte: From Jeremiah's leopard to today's analogous duck, there is a tragic consistency in man's character. Still tempted to hide or cover up our sinful nature, we, like the people of Jerusalem, avoid humble acceptance of our lost condition and prophetic destruction.

God has warned us through Jeremiah that "a leopard doesn't change its spots." He can see our true sinful character and calls us to repentance.

Thankfully, through God's Son, man's character *can* be changed, not with a feigned outward mask but with a new spiritual nature created through faith in Christ. While we can't change "our spots" by ourselves, Christ, who bore our sins on the cross, can cleanse the blemish created by our sins."Though your sins can be scarlet, they shall be as white as snow" (Isaiah 1:18).

If the fabric of your life is still spoiled by sin's spots, permit Christ to bathe you in His love and forgiveness. Only He can get those spots out.

Led Down the Garden Path

Matthew 26:46

Today's Phrase: Several references date the figurative expression "led down the garden path" to First World War vintage. A 1926 book entitled *Sounding Brass*, by Ethel Mannin, suggests it comes from flirting or teasing girls who "led soldiers down the garden path only to refuse what comes naturally." It is true that today's popular usage of the expression "led down the garden path," implies betrayal and deception; but I submit that the Bible is a more likely origin.

Biblical Background: Matthew 26 relates the episode of Christ's betrayal in the Garden of Gethsemane. Christ, assembled with several disciples in the garden, prayed as they peacefully slept. The stillness abruptly ended when Judas, one of the twelve disciples, led a band of Roman soldiers into their midst and betrayed Jesus into the hands of the Roman captors with a kiss.

It's clear that Judas led the captors "down the garden path" on a mission of betrayal and deception. His treachery resulted in the ultimate trial and crucifixion of the Savior, Jesus Christ.

Bible Byte: Maybe the scholars are right, and it's only coincidence that today's expression fits the biblical context of Judas's betrayal. The academic argument is of little consequence. My purpose is not to win scholarly debate, and I don't want to lead any reader "down the garden path." But there is a path you *should* know about. It's the safest path, one which follows Christ. As the Bible teaches, "Thy word is a lamp unto my feet, and a light unto my path" (Psalm 119:105). With Christ, you cannot be misled.

Live Off the Fat of the Land

Genesis 45:18

Today's Phrase: Early American pioneers were a hearty breed. There were no microwave ovens or fast-food drive-throughs for them. Through hard and husky work, they subdued this rugged country. As they tamed the frontier, they learned to "live off the fat of the land." The background and origin of this phrase is recorded in Genesis 45.

Biblical Background: Severe famine was foretold for Egypt through Joseph's interpretation of Pharaoh's dreams. God revealed through Joseph that Pharaoh must store one-fifth of the harvest during seven years of plenty as a hedge against the impending seven-year famine. Pharaoh, realizing Joseph's wisdom was godly, appointed him ruler of the land of Egypt; and Joseph carried out God's revealed plan.

Following the seven years of abundance, famine consumed the land. Famished people cried unto Pharaoh for bread, but he had delegated complete control of the storehouse to Joseph. Joseph, originally sold as a slave into Egypt by his jealous brothers, had miraculously become extremely powerful, and all nations had to negotiate with him to purchase food. This remarkable chain of events sets the stage for Joseph's reunion with his father and eleven brothers.

As the family of Joseph departed famine-wracked Canaan, they headed to Egypt to purchase food. While they all had long ago assumed Joseph was dead, a wonderful reunion of this family and Joseph's ultimate forgiveness of his brothers are depicted in Genesis 42:1–46:12. Joseph wisely acknowledged that while his brothers' deed had been meant for evil, God had providentially directed it for good.

Pharaoh, pleased to reward Joseph's faithful service, eagerly welcomed his newly reunited family into the land of Egypt: "I will give you the good of the land of Egypt, and ye shall eat the fat of the land" (Genesis 45:18).

Bible Byte: As this story in Genesis reveals, "the fat of the land" in Egypt had not come easily. Only through faithful diligence to God's instruction was it abundant during a time of great need. Similarly, our pioneer forefathers paid a great price to extract the fat of this land. History records one great motivation spurring the development of this country was the pursuit of religious freedom. Clearly, God rewarded that faithful pursuit with abundant blessings.

Thankfully, we today still enjoy a land of plenty. But we have another "fat" as well. It's the "fat" of self-indulgence. We're fat with convenience, fat with leisure time, and even fat with apathy. It's a sobering consideration, or should be. Let's not forget our abundance comes from God and He is worthy of our diligent service.

The Left Hand Doesn't Know What the Right Hand Is Doing

Matthew 6:4

Today's Phrase: A frequent problem in large business is poor communication between departments. Surprisingly, there's an almost traditional rift between the sales and service departments. Many times the poor customer gets caught in the middle of these communication miscues. The sales department promises a certain performance for their product, and invariably, the serviceman who comes to fix the problem says, "Oh, it isn't designed to do that." In frustration, the customer laments, "Don't you people talk to one another? Seems to me the left hand doesn't know what the right hand is doing."

Communication problems aren't limited to business. Lack of communication is a huge problem today, from corporate boardrooms to family bedrooms. Whether coworkers, family members, or marriage partners, those we're most close to often don't know our intent. And, most often, it's because we haven't communicated it to them. Our "left hand" doesn't know what the "right hand" is up to.

Interestingly, Christ originally suggested such lack of awareness might be a good idea. Let's examine His motive in prescribing such a recommendation.

Biblical Background: Christ's intention is clearly expressed in Matthew 6:1–4: "Take heed that ye do not your alms before men, to be seen of them: otherwise you have no reward of your Father which is in heaven. Therefore when thou doest thine alms, do not sound a trumpet before thee, as the hypocrites do in the synagogues and in the streets, that they may have glory of men. Verily I say unto you, They have their reward. But when thou doest alms, let not thy left hand know what thy right hand doeth: That thine alms may be in secret: and thy Father which seeth in secret himself shall reward thee openly."

Bible Byte: Today's colloquial phrase is virtually verbatim from ancient scripture. Yet again, colloquial usage has subtly distorted Christ's original intent. He had not intended to prevent effective verbal communication but rather to admonish against the human tendency to "self-promote." We are often eager to tell or show others how good we are. But, of course, God sees the internal motive.

Christ calls us to actions with pure motives. Service with intent to reap personal reward is nothing more than self-service. And Christ, who sits on the right hand of God, *always* knows what we are doing and why. Let's not worry about man's recognition. Concern yourself with service to others. If we take care of the "left hand," the "right hand of God," Jesus Christ, will take care of everything else.

Land of Milk and Honey

Exodus 3:8

Today's Phrase: America has long been recognized as a land of plenty. Fertile coastal valleys, rich Midwestern plains, and rocky New England dairies provide rich testimony of this nation's abundance. Today, a famine-plagued world is awed by the wealth of resources we enjoy; and immigrants for centuries have viewed this land as "the land of milk and honey."

The origin of this symbolic expression is God's call to the nation of Israel and His leading the Israelite people out of Egyptian bondage. It's recorded in Exodus.

Biblical Background: Speaking with Moses, God says, "I have surely seen the affliction of my people which are in Egypt, and have heard their cry by reason of their taskmasters; for I know their sorrows; And I am come down to deliver them out of the hand of the Egyptians, and to bring them up out of that land unto a good land and a large, unto a land flowing with milk and honey" (Exodus 3:7–8).

Bible Byte: Today, we colloquially employ the phrase "land of milk and honey" as a symbol of blessing and abundance. And certainly, America is indeed a "good and large land," richly blessed by God. We must also recognize, just as God called His people out of captivity in Egypt unto a generous land prepared for them, He calls each of us *individually* today. He hears the cries and sorrow of people *everywhere* and calls us out from the captivity of sin to a heavenly home, one prepared especially for His people. Consider the generous blessings enjoyed today in this "land of milk and honey" and look forward to the unimaginable blessings of heaven. Believe in Him, and someday He'll lead you there.

The Letter of the Law

2 Corinthians 3:6

Today's Phrase: We live in a nation of rules and standards, a nation of laws. We also are a people prone to find shortcuts. It's very common to ask, "Isn't that good enough?" We're always looking for an easier way or a means to just get by. Sometimes, the standards are not flexible.

"Not according to the letter of the law," is a typical response that illustrates the popular usage of this expression. In other words, a higher standard has been set, and if we don't measure up to it, it simply isn't good enough. Paul's second letter to Corinth is the origin for this phrase. It suggests we can never measure up to the standard set by the "letter of the law."

Biblical Background: Bible commentaries note that, in 2 Corinthians 3, Paul deals with the accreditation of the ministry. He begins with a question: "Do I need a letter of commendation certifying I am called to be one of God's ministers?" He answers his own question: "No, you as believers, are my letter of commendation. Not written in ink, or on tables of stone, but written by the Spirit of God on fleshly tables of the heart" (2 Corinthians 3:2–3).

In other words, Corinthian believers are the manifestation of Paul's ministry and are known by all men. Paul then contrasts his ministry of the new covenant with Christ to the Old Testament covenant embodied in the law of Moses: "Not that we are sufficient of ourselves … but our sufficiency is of God; Who also hath made us able ministers of the new testament; not of the letter, but of the spirit: for the letter killeth, but the spirit giveth life" (2 Corinthians 3:5–6).

Paul says, "We preach the new covenant with Christ, not the old covenant of laws. The law condemns, but the spirit saves."

Bible Byte: The Old Testament law, specifically the Ten Commandments, spells out death to man. No one can measure up to its requirements. Not even Moses, a murderer, or David, an adulterer and murderer, could keep the law. The law reveals we are sinners, falling short of God's higher standard. Though we might be prone to try to "just get by," God's standard will measure our shortfall every time.

Thankfully, we have a new promise in Christ, who doesn't condemn us but saves us from our sins. He's the only man ever to successfully live "by the letter of the law," God's law. Without Him, we will never be good enough.

Lip Service

Matthew 15:8

Today's Phrase: From trendy health spas to neighborhood sidewalks, fitness freaks are fashionably stretching and straining their bodies into condition; and *everyone* is talking about exercise. But, while fitness is in and fatness is out, great majorities of people are still only *talking* about exercise. Though many pay "lip service" to it, the actual commitment remains elusive.

Jesus observed that same lack of commitment in a spiritual sense and upbraided those hypocrites whose actions spoke louder than their words. Matthew contains His charge against the hypocritical Pharisees.

Biblical Background: "This people draweth nigh unto me with their mouth, and honoureth me with their lips, but their heart is far from me" (Matthew 15:8).

Bible Byte: Today's fitness craze provides an intriguing analogy to Christ's example. Certainly, there are many dedicated fitness buffs who are totally disciplined and committed to exercise, health foods, and aerobic conditioning. But there are just as many who use exercise and "working out" as a tool to mask the pitfalls of living to excess. These people tend to work out Monday through Thursday and "party out" on the weekends. The commitment is not to the lifestyle of fitness but to the outward appearance of fitness. Living the Christian life only on Sundays is a similar part-time commitment Jesus warned against.

Obviously, just as talking fitness won't improve physical conditioning, spiritual "lip service" can't improve our soul's condition. God wants our personal commitment, whole-hearted service, not empty "lip service." Clearly, Christ's words challenge all Christians to put their sweats on and get in spiritual shape.

Miss the Boat

Genesis 6:5–7:24

Today's Phrase: A recent ad in the local paper read, "Don't miss the boat on our super deals … best prices of the year! Buy now!" I was intrigued, but not by the ad. You see those types of pressure sales promotions every day. I was intrigued by the warning "don't miss the boat."

Obviously, it had nothing to do with cars. I'd heard this warning hundreds of times before relating to many kinds of products. So where does it come from? The phrase is not found in scripture, but it is found in context within the old, old Genesis account of Noah and the Flood. This story may well be the basis from which the first warning, "don't miss the boat," was sounded.

Biblical Background: In Genesis 6, the story begins. The wickedness and evil of man's heart grieved the Lord. He was sorry He had created man. The Lord decided to destroy all life on earth. Only Noah and his family found grace in God's eyes. Noah built an ark as commanded by God and eventually he, his family, and a whole zoo of animals were safely sheltered inside the ark as the floodwaters rose to cover the earth. It's, of course, a familiar tale. Those who observed Noah and his sons build the ark scoffed at them. After all, he was far from any water. His obedience appeared foolish. But we can well imagine their terror as the floodwaters rose to cover the mountains. (Genesis 7:20) The final commentary on those who "missed the boat" is contained in verse 23: "And every living substance was destroyed which was upon the face of the ground … and Noah only remained alive, and they that were with him in the ark."

Bible Byte: Today, when we "miss the boat," the consequences may be trivial. So what if I "miss the boat" on some special promotion? I really don't need a new car. But, clearly, to "miss the boat" in Noah's time was a serious mistake. While God promised to never again destroy the earth with a flood, an inevitable judgment still looms ahead for this world. The warning has been sounded. Just as there was safety within the ark, today, there is safety in Christ. The door of grace is still open. Don't be late. Come on board before the door is forever closed.

Man of Few Words

Proverbs 17:27

Today's Phrase: I'm a quiet individual by nature; some would say reserved and measured in conversation. Perhaps I learned this from my father who often said, "It's better to be silent and thought a fool than to open your mouth and remove all doubt."

I'm not sure who first coined that phrase, but clearly, it contains a high degree of wisdom. In today's world where everyone is eager to tell you what they know, there seems to be a certain respect earned by a "man of few words." At one time I was self-conscious about my reserved nature, that is, until I discovered this principle, and this phrase, originated in ancient scripture.

Biblical Background: "He that hath knowledge spareth his words: and a man of understanding is of an excellent spirit. Even a fool, when he holdeth his peace, is counted wise: and he that shutteth his lips is esteemed a man of understanding" (Proverbs 17:27–28).

Bible Byte: Clearly, the Bible is the basis for both my father's advice and today's popular colloquial expression. Considering that I profess to be a "man of few words," I've probably said enough; but one more thing should be noted: "The fool hath said in his heart, There is no God" (Psalm 14:1).

Don't be foolish. Open your mouth and confess Jesus Christ. Those are words each of us must *not* be reluctant to proclaim.

Made Light of It

Matthew 22:5

Today's Phrase: It can be a crushing blow when a group of friends don't take you seriously. You might think, "Hey, I've got something important to say." But, once expressed, if your peers "made light of it," you feel pretty foolish. It can happen to anyone, and Matthew records an incident where even a *king* wasn't taken seriously.

Biblical Background: Matthew 22 presents another of Jesus's parables. Jesus explains: "The kingdom of heaven is like unto a certain king, which made a marriage for his son, And sent forth his servants to call them that were bidden to the wedding: and they would not come" (Matthew 22:2–3).

The king's invited guests would not come. Perhaps they were too busy, but they weren't even considerate enough to RSVP. Still, the king implored them again: "Again, he sent forth other servants, saying, Tell them which are bidden, Behold, I have prepared my dinner … all things are ready: come unto the marriage" (Matthew 22:4).

But again, his guests ignored him: "But they made light of it, and went their ways, one to his farm, another to his merchandise" (Matthew 22:5).

Obviously, they didn't take the king seriously. In fact, as the story continues, some of the invited guests got so irritated with the king that they killed his servants. When the king discovered their deed, he sent his armies to destroy both the murderers and their cities. These ungrateful guests proved unworthy, so the king then sent his servants to the streets. "Go ye therefore into the highways, and as many as ye shall find, bid to the marriage" (Matthew 22:9).

The servants responded by bringing anyone they could find to the wedding. Eventually, the guest list was filled. Yet, even some of these were unworthy: "And when the king came in to see the guests, he saw there a man which had not on a wedding garment: And he saith unto him, Friend, how camest thou in hither not having a wedding garment? And he was speechless. Then said the king to the servants, Bind him hand and foot, and take him away … For many are called, but few are chosen" (Matthew 22:11–14).

Bible Byte: Eventually, the king's guest list was trimmed to the right and acceptable few. Those who "made light of it" and rejected his feast were destroyed. Those coming unprepared were likewise thrown out. And in both cases, they were speechless. The king's offer was something to be taken seriously. It's a picture of Christ's offer today. Come, and join Him. You're invited. But remember to prepare yourself. It's not something to "make light of."

My Two Cents

Luke 21:1–4

Today's Phrase: People typically "give their two cents" in a negative context. "My opinion may not be worth much, but here's my two cents anyway, for what it's worth."

Obviously, at face value, two cents do not represent much worth today. Two copper coins simply command little, if any, influence. Yet, two copper coins in Jesus's time, though also of meager monetary worth, were considered much more valuable than many larger sums by the Lord.

Biblical Background: In Luke 21:1–4, Jesus observed a poor widow offering a gift of two mites to the church treasury and praised her generosity. History records a mite as the smallest Jewish coin. Made of copper, it had very little monetary worth, just as our copper penny today. But Jesus differentiated the value of her gift by focusing on motive and commitment, not monetary worth. The rich gave from their abundance, but the widow gave in spite of her extreme needs. Clearly, her "two cents worth" was of considerable value in His eyes.

Bible Byte: The widow's two copper coins have become "my two cents" in today's colloquial expression. Unfortunately, familiar usage of the phrase today tends to *discount* worth by focusing on face value. "It's not worth much, but here's my two cents."

Face value, however, is not at all what Jesus considered. He emphasized the true worth, the heart and motive behind the act. The widow gave unpretentiously, genuinely, probably never realizing her act was observed. Yet, she lives forever in the pages of scripture, providing a priceless lesson about giving and selflessness. Such purity of motive is a rich lesson from two copper coins, isn't it? Consider it, for what it's worth.

Not Fit for Man or Beast

Jeremiah 51:62

Today's Phrase: I used to love cold, snowy days as a kid. I could count on school closing for the day; and we kids would romp and frolic in the crisp, wintry air building forts and tossing snowballs. My mom would always warn me, "Bundle up good, Billy! It's not fit for man or beast outside today." The prophet Jeremiah also spoke of a land "not fit for man or beast." It wasn't due to weather; but in a way, the spiritual climate of the day was involved.

Biblical Background: Jeremiah is often called the "weeping prophet." He gets this label from his prophetic writings. God's message for the people of that day, delivered through Jeremiah, broke his heart. He told of the coming destruction of Jerusalem and eventual captivity of Israel in the Babylonian empire. Jeremiah's writings are characterized by his message of warning against backsliding. The term "backsliding" refers to a return to sin and is mentioned more in Jeremiah than in any other book: "Thine own wickedness shall correct thee, and thy backslidings shall reprove thee: know … that thou hast forsaken the LORD thy God" (Jeremiah 2:19).

Babylon was a great power in those days and did, in fact, overcome a spiritually backslid Jerusalem, taking her citizens into captivity. But near the end of his writings, Jeremiah gives a prophecy of destruction and judgment to the great world power of Babylon as well. Jeremiah foretells Babylon's fall from power and the return of the children of

Israel to their God. Jeremiah writes of Babylon, "Because of the wrath of the LORD it shall not be inhabited, but it shall be wholly desolate: every one that goeth by Babylon shall be astonished, and hiss at all her plagues" (Jeremiah 50:13).

And chapter 51 continues, "O LORD, thou hast spoken against this place, to cut it off, that none shall remain in it, neither man nor beast, but that it shall be desolate for ever" (Jeremiah 51:62). Remarkably, these prophecies have seen literal fulfillment, as any tourist to the Babylonian ruins will attest.

Bible Byte: My mom's warning was given to protect me from the harshness of a cold wintry day. She would have preferred I remain in the warmth and protection of the house because she knew I'd likely take off my scarf or hat and loose some of the protection she'd provided.

Jeremiah's prophecy to the nation Israel was also one of concern. He agonized over his backslid people, seeing that as they let their guard down, they were out of God's protection. Without fellowship with God, they would eventually fall into sin. And the consequences of that sin were Israel's captivity.

We are captives as well, captive to our sin nature. But Christ calls us into the warmth and security of His love. While the power and appeal of sin is great, it has been defeated. At the day of final judgment, Satan and his legions will be cast into total desolation, into an "outer darkness" not fit for man or beast. Don't stay out in the cold. Come into the warmth of Christ's open arms.

Once and for All

2 Corinthians 5:15
Romans 6:10

Today's Phrase: To be honest, I'm a pretty competitive guy. I've long since given up organized sports, but I really don't need an organized competition to challenge myself. It can be something as simple as tossing a wad of paper at a garbage pail across the room. Like a kid, I'll sit there and toss it over and over until I get it and usually invent some crazy sports challenge out of it, to boot.

To my family, I must seem obsessed. Many times my wife has pleaded with me to stop, but I just can't. I have to practice over and over again until I master it. I put her off with some pleading of my own: "Honey, I've just gotta get this thing once and for all."

To her dismay and annoyance, however, I usually keep at it until I get it not just once, but over and over again. As if driven, I keep going until I master it repeatedly. Though I say I'll do it "once," I don't really mean that at all.

Another word in this expression is also ignored, the word "all." Typically, when I get caught up in one of these silly self-challenges, I'm not doing it for anyone other than *myself*. Yet, my expression of determination says "once and for all." Clearly I'm not doing it just "once" and certainly am not doing it for "all." While my meaning doesn't come close to what the words literally say, biblical usage of the expression means *precisely* that.

<u>Biblical Background</u>: In Paul's letter to the Romans, he writes, "Knowing that Christ being raised from the dead dieth no more; death hath no more dominion over him. For in that he died, he died unto sin *once*"(Romans 6:9–10).

In Paul's letter to the believers at Corinth he states, "And that he died for all" (2 Corinthians 5:15).

<u>Bible Byte</u>: Today's expression implies a sort of persistence. We might say "once and for all" but really mean "I'm gonna do it 'til I master it!" and "I'm doing it for myself!" The biblical context means exactly what it says. Christ died "once and for all," for you and for me. He paid our sin penalty by dying in our place. Thank God. And the next time you're determined to master something "once and for all," remember, only the Lord Jesus Christ really did.

Out of the Mouths of Babes

Psalm 8:2
Matthew 21:16

<u>Today's Phrase</u>: Sometimes, it takes a child's innocent perspective to unmask the folly of adults. That's what is meant by the phrase "out of the mouths of babes." To my embarrassment, I will relate a personal example.

Recently, I almost made a very foolish purchase based solely on rationalization. I really wanted a grand piano. Now admittedly, that's not so bad; but I was willing to use funds that I had previously set aside for the children's education to get it. The money wasn't there from other sources, and I was all too eager to rationalize away my previous "hands-off" policy toward college savings just to manipulate the purchase. It took my youngest son, Bobby, with all the wisdom and insight only a seven-year-old can muster, to cut through to my selfishness.

"I don't get it, Dad," he questioned. "You already have a good piano. What's so special about the *shape* of the new one?" Bobby had observed my struggles to rationalize this purchase, had overheard my discussions regarding finances, and, quite innocently, saw that we already had a perfectly good piano of a different shape in the living room. He couldn't understand why I'd do something so obviously contradictory. When his question came out, my eyes met my wife's. I muttered, "Out of the mouths of babes." We both recognized his innocent question for what it was. Clearly, Bobby saw my selfish motives.

Biblical Background: The intellectual wisdom of man can get in the way of innocent acceptance of spiritual truths. Passages in both Psalms and Matthew reveal this condition:

"Out of the mouth of babes and sucklings hast thou ordained strength" (Psalm 8:2).

"Out of the mouth of babes and sucklings thou hast perfected praise" (Matthew 21:16).

In both cases, biblical context suggests that God does not act in a way people would expect. It is not the wise or the mighty who God seeks but rather the helpless and weak. God wants us to rely on Him, not on ourselves. Scripture teaches that God is not a respecter of persons. (Romans 2:11) God is not impressed with those things by which people measures themselves or others. God reveals himself unto those with a childlike innocence, without pretense. He makes these souls strong and wise as they grow in reliance on Him.

Bible Byte: It's true, little Bobby didn't fully appreciate the deep tones and rich beauty of a fine grand piano. (And that's not rationalization again.) But he certainly *did* see the obvious manipulation and rationalization I struggled through to justify getting what I wanted. His innocent question changed my mind. Oh, I still *want* one, but I'm not willing to jeopardize other family *needs* to obtain it. I'll trust in the Lord, who supplies over and above my needs, that one day I may receive it. And, thanks to Bobby, I received some very valuable counsel, out of the mouths of babes, in the meantime.

Pulled It Out of the Fire

Jude 1:23

Today's Phrase: I'm a baseball fan, a *Chicago Cubs* baseball fan. (Now, I know there are skeptics who label "Cubs baseball" an oxymoron. Like "jumbo shrimp," for example, the words *Cubs* and *baseball* are arguably contradictory terms.) Yet, for all their foibles and follies, I'm still a fan. And any longtime Cub fan will well understand why I'm just as defiantly *not* a New York Mets fan. As a Christian, I'm to forgive, but I'm afraid I shall never forget the 1969 National League pennant race between *my* Cubs and those New York Mets.

Suffice it to say, New York won. They should have been losers, but they won. They literally "pulled it out of the fire." Defying all the odds, overcoming all but certain defeat, and narrowly escaping the pit of despair, the Mets won. They were victorious. And, like the solitary pennant claimed by the Cubs, also ancient history, the solitary chapter of Jude provides the illustration from which we derive today's expression "pulled it out of the fire." It, too, is an illustration of narrow escape; but as you might guess, this victory is no mere game.

Biblical Background: Jude is a bold book, small in volume, yet high in impact. It's a pragmatic "rubber-meets-the-road" book. It warns Christians to be diligent, to "earnestly contend for the faith" (Jude 1:3). Its basic message: You can't be lax and believe, cannot be cavalier and Christian. And it warns of the coming apostasy in latter days, when believers will drift away from God. While some people view Christians as meek and mild, Jude's warning suggests the Christian faith is not a pursuit for the weak or fainthearted.

The Christian life is a struggle, if not a battle, against the snares of evil, not just evil from without, but evils from within. Jude warns that deceitful God-mockers will infiltrate the church in latter days. They will sound like and look the part of true believers but are treacherous entrapments for the unwary warrior.

"But, beloved, remember ye the words which were spoken before of the apostles … How that they told you there should be mockers in the last time, who should walk after their own ungodly lusts. These be they who separate themselves, sensual, having not the Spirit. But ye, beloved, building up yourselves on your most holy faith, praying in the Holy Ghost, Keep yourselves in the love of God, looking for the mercy of our Lord Jesus Christ unto eternal life. And of some have compassion, making a difference: And others save with fear, pulling them out of the fire" (Jude 1:17–23).

Bible Byte: Jude challenges Christians to make a difference. Fight not only to maintain your own faith, but with boldness and compassion, fight to save others from the flaming pit of hell. Christianity is not a game. Nor is it a life for the fainthearted. It's a fight. But to be victorious is to gain eternal life. Not that we win it ourselves. Only through the miraculous rescue of Christ is the victory claimed. And, after the final "out," it's the only victory pennant worth winning.

Peter Out

Matthew 26:26–75

Today's Phrase: Life styles today play out at a torrid pace. "Life in the fast lane," we say. This slogan implies we are really moving. But are we getting anywhere? The hectic schedules in my family make my head spin. Sometimes it's overwhelming. I can't keep up. The stress gets the best of me, and I "peter out."

This very popular phrase means to give out gradually or to diminish over time. Often we use it to excuse disappointment, such as when we let someone down. "Sorry, I peter'd out on you," we might say. This expression comes from the Gospel account of Peter's denial of Christ.

Biblical Background: The setting for the time of Peter's denial was near the end of Christ's ministry, just prior to Judas's betrayal. During their Last Supper together, Jesus explained the coming events to His disciples. After sharing communion with His closest followers, He stated, "All ye shall be offended because of me this night" (Matthew 26:31).

But Peter impulsively replied, "Though all men shall be offended because of thee, yet will I never be offended" (Matthew 26:33).

Jesus, knowingly told Peter that before the rooster would crow on the morrow, he would deny Him three times. Peter again rebuked the Lord, "Though I should die with thee, yet will I not deny thee" (Matthew 26:35).

Within a matter of hours, Judas's treachery yielded its fruit, and Jesus was carried away into captivity. The mockery of a trial and Christ's cruel torture began as Peter sat outside the palace. A young girl in the crowd thought she recognized Peter as one she had seen with Jesus. Peter denied it. He stood up and moved away from the girl. But another recognized him and asked if he knew Jesus. He denied it again, this time with an oath, probably saying, "I swear, I don't know this man!" Soon, others came by and said, "Surely thou also art one of them." Peter cursed and adamantly denied Christ for the third time. Matthew 26:74–75 records the picture: "And immediately the cock crew. And Peter remembered the word of Jesus … And he went out, and wept bitterly."

Bible Byte: Peter's disappointment was deep. He had not only let Christ down, but he had hurt himself. He had denied fellowship and his relationship with Christ. He felt bitterness, loss, and shame.

We, too, will feel that loss without Christ in our lives. And in this hectic world, it's all too easy to leave our relationship with Him for last. You can always count on Him. Can He count on you? It can be tough, but don't peter out. Hang in there. You'll be glad you did.

The Powers That Be

Romans 13:1

Today's Phrase: While working as a field representative for a large corporation, I lived far removed from the corporate world. I was on the front lines, where the action was. The bureaucracy was comfortably far away. We field reps coined an expression that described the autonomy we sometimes had to exercise: "It's easier to beg forgiveness than to ask for permission." It was simply easier to act than explain. And the pace in the "trenches" demanded rapid commercial action. It might have been more politically prudent to check with "the powers that be" back at headquarters, but it wasn't always feasible.

Paul's letter to the Romans is the origin for the expression "the powers that be." But Paul sheds an interesting light on the source of all authority and the importance of submitting to it.

Biblical Background: Paul writes to believers at Rome, and certainly many of those believers were Jewish. However, as Jews, they were subject to Roman rule and authority. Most resented the oppressive Roman government. Paul's letter admonishes them to obey those in authority regardless, for even if the government were ruled by wicked and evil men, God is still in control: "Let every soul be subject unto the higher powers. For there is no power but of God: the powers that be are ordained of God" (Romans 13:1).

Bible Byte: As one considers the "powers that be" in this day and age, it seems unlikely that they are ordained of God. To be subject unto authority today is therefore perhaps a puzzling admonition in light of the corruption rampant in many governments. But neither government nor any man has an authority that is not granted or allowed by God. And while we may not understand God's plan, He is on the throne and in control.

God ordains the "powers that be," but He is the ultimate, final authority. Be sure to check with Him. And, if you've acted on your own, without His direction, you can still seek His guidance. It's simple. Just ask His forgiveness. Pray to the only true and ultimate "powers that be," the Father, Son, and Holy Spirit.

From Pillar to Post

Matthew 27:26
Mark 15:15

Today's Phrase: After a thorough search for a lost article, you might hear someone say, "I went from pillar to post but just couldn't find it." Quite an odd expression, isn't it? Some references suggest this expression relates to boundaries in the game of tennis; but I suspect it has more ancient, scriptural roots.

Biblical Background: Following Christ's betrayal, He was taken before Pontius Pilate and tried in the Roman court. The Jews claimed He had blasphemed God; but because the Jews were under Roman rule, they were not able to kill Christ under the authority of Mosaic law alone. They appealed to Pontius Pilate, charging Christ with the offense of treason, citing Christ's claim to be king of the Jews as evidence of His treason to Roman authority.

Though Pilate found no fault in Jesus, he was politically pressured into delivering Christ to be crucified. Both Matthew and Mark relate the event:

"When he (Pilate) had scourged Jesus, he delivered him to be crucified" (Matthew 27:26).

"And so Pilate, willing to content the people … delivered Jesus, when he had scourged him, to be crucified" (Mark 15:15).

The Roman punishment of scourging was gruesome. It was common for a criminal to lean upon a column or pillar while being beaten with a shredded leather whip. Many strands of the whip were tied to lead pieces or jagged glass, so the blows to the back viciously ripped and slashed the skin.

The penalty of crucifixion was even more horrible. Christ, our Savior, hung on a post like the lowest common criminal of His time. Could it be that "from pillar to post" relates not at all to tennis but to the gruesome and cruel suffering endured by our Lord at the hands of men?

Bible Byte: I believe there is quite possibly a connection between today's phrase and Christ's ancient suffering. Today's common phrase implies to "go all out" or "go to all extremes." Certainly, Christ endured to the ultimate, giving His life. Perhaps I can't prove the colloquial correlation, but I do know whenever I hear the phrase "from pillar to post," I'll immediately think of Christ's suffering. And I'll remember that the extremes of Christ's example could never be matched. More importantly, I know it doesn't *have* to be matched. Christ paid my sin debt in full. He went all out, from His scourging at the pillar to His death upon Calvary's post.

Put Words in My Mouth

2 Samuel 14:3

Today's Phrase: "Don't put words in my mouth. That's not what I said." Chances are, you've expressed these exact words at some time. We've all been the victims of misinterpretation or embellishment of something we've said, especially when someone can slightly twist our words to confirm their own sentiments or achieve their own ends.

This old trick has been going on for centuries. The Old Testament book of 2 Samuel originates the phrase in a story beginning in chapter 13. It's a long story but fascinating. Lust, rape, scandal, murder, and deceit fill its pages. It rivals any modern soap opera for suspense and intrigue.

Biblical Background: First, let's meet the characters of this complex tale:

David	King of Israel
Absalom	Son of David
Amnon	Absalom's brother
Tamar	Absalom's beautiful sister
Jonadab	King David's nephew and cousin to David's children
Joab	David's servant
A woman of Tekoah	Her name is never revealed

The tale unfolds with the revelation that Amnon is lovesick for his beautiful and virtuous sister, Tamar. Amnon realized he couldn't have her, and he grew depressed by the day. Cousin Jonadab noticed Amnon's behavior and persuaded him to confide his dilemma. Jonadab, described as a subtle or crafty man, devised a plan for Amnon to be alone with Tamar: "And Jonadab said unto him, Lay thee down on thy bed, and make thyself sick: and when thy Father cometh to see thee, say unto him, I pray thee, let my sister Tamar come, and give me meat, and dress the meat in my sight, that I may see it, and eat it at her hand" (2 Samuel 13:5).

Yes, this boy had it bad. He was going to feign sickness to manipulate an opportunity to be alone with Tamar. And he wanted to watch her cook. As you may suspect, Jonadab's advice also involved other plans.

The plan unfolds without a hitch. But, after Tamar prepared the food, Amnon refused to eat. He sent every male servant away and invited Tamar into his bed chamber, so she could feed him. Tamar complied, perhaps thinking that Amnon was so weak he could not feed himself. As she approached the bed, Amnon grabbed her: "He took hold of her, and said unto her, Come lie with me, my sister" (2 Samuel 13:11). But Tamar, of course, refused: "And she answered him, Nay, my brother, do not force me; for no such thing ought to be done in Israel: do not thou this folly" (2 Samuel 13:12).

She pleaded with him, even suggesting that if Amnon appealed to their father, King David, he would not prevent their marriage. However, Amnon was so overcome with lust that he raped his own sister: "Howbeit he would not hearken unto her voice: but, being stronger than she, forced her, and lay with her" (2 Samuel 13:14).

Predictably, once Amnon had his way with Tamar, his "love" turned sour. Feeling both guilt and shame, he now despised her: "Then Amnon hated her exceedingly; so that the hatred wherewith he hated her was greater than the love wherewith he had loved her. And Amnon said unto her, Arise, be gone" (2 Samuel 13:15).

He called unto his servant and had Tamar thrown out of his chamber. She was humiliated and ashamed. Absalom, her brother, saw her crying and sensed her distress immediately. Clearly, he must have been feeling the lecherous vibes of Amnon.

"And Absalom her brother said unto her, Hath Amnon thy brother been with thee?" (2 Samuel 13:20).

Absalom comforted Tamar and took her into his home. He would not speak to Amnon and told Tamar to likewise divulge the deed to no one. "Hold now thy peace, my sister: he is thy brother; regard not this thing" (2 Samuel 13:20).

Still, King David did find out. Although he was very angry, scriptures do not tell us that King David ever did anything about it. Incredibly, in fact, nothing apparently was done to punish Amnon. Yet Absalom grew to hate Amnon for what he had done.

Two full years passed. Apparently, everyone had brushed this ugly episode under the carpet, that is, all but Absalom and Tamar.

Absalom plotted to kill Amnon. His scheme was carried out by servants who killed Amnon one evening when Amnon was "merry with wine" (2 Samuel 13:28). King David heard of the killing and wept with mourning, while Absalom fled to another part of the country. Three more years passed by. King David longed to see his son Absalom, for this estrangement from his beloved son was like having two dead boys, and he ached for Absalom to return. But Absalom was a murderer, and under Mosaic law was banished. King David knew he could not restore Absalom to his position in the family, for the family would demand Absalom's death as punishment.

Again David did not act, though his heart ached. The stage had been set for Joab, King David's servant, and an unnamed woman from the village of Tekoah to intervene. Joab realized King David longed for Absalom, and he devised a plan to manipulate their reunion: "And Joab sent to Tekoah, and fetched thence a wise woman, and said unto her, I pray thee, feign thyself to be a mourner, and put on now mourning apparel, and anoint not thyself with oil, but be as a woman that had a long time mourned for the dead: And come to the king, and speak on this manner unto him. So Joab put the words in her mouth" (2 Samuel 14:2–3).

Joab "put words in her mouth." He crafted a cunning tale and rehearsed it with the woman of Tekoah. She came before King David, as Joab had planned, and appealed to him for help: "And the king said unto her, What aileth thee? And she answered, I am indeed a widow woman, and mine husband is dead. And thy handmaid had two sons, and they two strove together in the field, and there was none to part them, but the one smote the other, and slew him. And, behold, the whole family is risen against thine handmaid, and they said, Deliver him that smote his brother, that we may kill him" (2 Samuel 14:5–7).

Sound familiar? Joab's story paralleled that of Absalom and Amnon. King David, though he would not react in his own family tragedy, finally reacted to this strange woman's story.

"And he said, As the LORD liveth, there shall not one hair of thy son fall to the earth" (2 Samuel 14:11).

Now Joab had him where he wanted him. King David has proclaimed safety for the son of this stranger. Now he must be made to see his own folly regarding Absalom's banishment. The woman of Tekoah then confronts the king with his personal situation, and finally the light came on for King David: "And the king said, Is not the hand of Joab with thee in all this?" (2 Samuel 14:19).

With the clever facade stripped away, Joab's involvement was clear.

"And the king said unto Joab, Behold now, I have done this thing: go therefore, bring the young man Absalom again" (2 Samuel 14:21).

"So Joab arose and went to Geshur, and brought Absalom to Jerusalem" (2 Samuel 14:23).

Bible Byte: Joab certainly "put words in her mouth." They were not meant to harm but to help. He saw how King David wept for Absalom, and his cunning plan ultimately reunited father and son. A key verse in this story is 2 Samuel 14:14. The wise woman of Tekoah, speaking to King David said, "For we must needs die, and are as water spilt on the ground, which cannot be gathered up again; neither doth God respect any person: yet doth he devise means, that his banished be not expelled from him" (2 Samuel 14:14).

Absalom's sin banished him from his father. And Joab's plan reunited father and son. Likewise, although we are God's children, sin banishes *us* from *our* Heavenly Father. But God's plan can also reunite us. He has devised a means whereby His banished and erring children need not be forever expelled. He has given us His Son, known in scripture as His Word. Don't merely put the "word" in your mouth; hide it in your *heart* as well. A joyous reunion awaits you.

Practice What You Preach

Matthew 23:3

Today's Phrase: What we parents say and what we actually do are not always a match. When my kids trap me in one of those behavioral contradictions, I'm always hit with a chorus of "C'mon, Dad, practice what you preach."

This admonition has been around for centuries, and it's likely that today's popular quote originates from a similar challenge issued by Christ to the religious authorities of His day.

Biblical Background: The Pharisees of the Holy City were highly visible figures. As the authorities in Israel, they were accorded great respect, even admiration. They were well educated and rooted in Mosaic aw and were often called "teacher" or even "master." No doubt this elevated stature inflated their egos. But, while they were highly qualified to teach the law, they were not at all able to "master" it.

Christ did not challenge their position, but He clearly confronted their behavior. He publicly upbraided the Pharisees for their outward piety and for their long and eloquent prayers in public places. He charged them with pretense, conceit, and hypocrisy. He said they might be able to preach the law but they could not practice it: "Then spake Jesus to the multitude, and to his disciples, Saying The scribes and Pharisees sit in Moses' seat: All therefore whatsoever they bid you observe, that observe and do; but do not ye after their works: for they say, and do not" (Matthew 23:1–3).

Bible Byte: Christ also taught in Matthew 23:11–12: "He that is greatest among you shall be your servant. And whosoever shall exalt himself shall be abased; and he that shall humble himself shall be exalted" (Matthew 23:11–12).

We don't need authority *figures*; we need servants in authority. We don't need papier-mâché characters, we need *characters* with solid values. Unfortunately, my kids probably haven't challenged the last contradiction between my parental preaching and my parental practice. But we parents must be mindful that our authority is not license to preach one thing while practicing another. The old saying of "walk the talk" applies. Your walk talks, and your talk talks; but your walk talks louder than your talk talks. Said more succinctly, we should practice what we preach.

Raise Cain

Genesis 4:2–16

Today's Phrase: After a hard week's work, most of us look forward to Friday and the weekend. For some, it's a time to relax, work in the garden, or spend time with the family. For many (we've coined the term "party animal"), it's a time to "raise Cain." Wild parties, loud music, and a little mischief are the stuff their weekends are made of. Why would that be called "raising Cain"? Let's look to the Genesis account of two brothers, Cain and Abel, to find out.

Biblical Background: Genesis 4:2–11, relate the story of the first brothers of the Bible. (And if you ever thought "sibling rivalry" was a modern phenomenon, think again.) Cain was the firstborn, a "tiller of the ground" or farmer. Abel was a "keeper of sheep" or shepherd. As an offering to the Lord, both boys gave of their labors. Cain gave "of the fruit of the ground," but Abel gave "of the firstlings of his flock and of the fat thereof." The implication that Abel gave the best he had is clear. Cain apparently held back, and though he was still making an offering, it was not an unselfish or sacrificial gift.

"And the LORD had respect unto Abel and to his offering: But unto Cain and to his offering he had not respect. And Cain was very wroth, and his countenance fell" (Genesis 4:4–5).

Cain's anger showed in his long face, but the Lord confronted Cain with his motive: "If thou doest well, shalt thou not be accepted? and if thou doest *not* well, sin lieth at the door" (Genesis 4:7).

Cain's anger was intense, and in a rage, he jealously killed his brother, Abel. The consequence of his murderous act was separation from God, a bitter end for a bitter man.

Bible Byte: After reading the story of these two brothers, it's difficult to imagine why anyone would want to revive that old selfish nature displayed by Cain. But it's clear why the expression "raising Cain," is synonymous with mischief and unrest. Clearly, Cain found no peace after his selfish deed. And his motive to hold back from God to do evil, resulted in "sin at the door." There is never any rest in that condition.

Have you ever noticed a "party animal" on a Monday? Do they look peaceful and rested? Hardly. The consequence of a riotous lifestyle takes a heavy toll on the body. They might "raise Cain" on Friday and Saturday, but they need to lie down on Sunday and Monday. More importantly, they ignore the opportunity for heavenly rest. Give God your best. Give Him your life, unselfishly. Make every day of the week something to look forward to.

Rise and Shine

Isaiah 60:1

Today's Phrase: I'm not a morning person, but high-energy morning people think everybody should be. They cheerfully, and quite honestly, rudely bubble over with the singsong *Rise and Shine.* It's maddening! I appreciate a cautious, measured entry into the morning. These high-energy morning people boldly, and usually loudly, catapult themselves into the day.

There is a day coming when everyone will be a "morning person," even I. Isaiah 60 explains the origin for the morning person's anthem *Rise and Shine.*

Biblical Background: Isaiah presents the prophecies of the Lord's second coming. Chapter 60 begins as a prophetic call for that triumphant day: "Arise, shine; for thy light is come, and the glory of the LORD is risen upon thee" (Isaiah 60:1).

"Thy light" refers to Jesus Christ, who is described in the New Testament as the light of the world.

"Then spake Jesus again unto them, saying, I am the light of the world: he that followeth me shall not walk in darkness, but shall have the light of life" (John 8:12).

Bible Byte: It has been said that "prophecy is the mold into which history is poured." Isaiah sets the mold. Jesus will come again, and the shadows and the darkness of sin, which so permeate our world, will be chased away by the light of His love. When He returns, it will be a brand-new day. And Christ, called the "bright and morning star" (Revelations 22:16), will light the way. Be ready. Be a "morning person." Rise and shine!

Reap What You Sow

Galatians 6:7

Today's Phrase: In our large family of five children, squabbles are unavoidable. We try to teach the kids kindness, but kids are prone to forget. And they do so with frustrating regularity. When it gets too out of hand, the kids can count on one of two speeches. They call one "the blood speech." That's my "How can you be so mean to your own flesh and blood?" lecture I've used so often. The other they call the "garden speech." That's my "you reap what you sow" speech. We talk about planting corn or watermelon or peas, which always leads to a harvest of corn, watermelon or peas. You can't sow corn and get watermelon. Likewise, when they "plant" kindness, they'll harvest it in return. Sometimes, this works. But I take no credit. It's not my original thought. Galatians contains the original use of the phrase "reap what you sow."

Biblical Background: Paul's letter to the Galatian church is straightforward and to the point. In Galatians 6:7–8, he writes, "Be not deceived; God is not mocked: for whatsoever a man soweth, that shall he also reap. For he that soweth to his flesh shall of the flesh reap corruption; but he that soweth to the Spirit shall of the Spirit reap life everlasting."

Bible Byte: People today have their priorities out of balance. There's an overemphasis on the temporal, and there is too much striving for material wealth and entertainment. The Bible states that these things will rot and decay. Only the spirit is eternal. Christ says, "Lay not up for yourselves treasures upon earth, where moth and rust doth corrupt, and where thieves break through and steal: But lay up for yourselves treasures in heaven … For where your treasure is, there will your heart be also" (Matthew 6:19–21).

We reap what we sow. And the party life doesn't yield much of value. Plant your heart in heaven and grow in the spirit of God. And when God reaps the harvest of souls, you'll be among His precious fruit.

Sparks Are Gonna Fly

Job 5:7

Today's Phrase: Anyone who reads a daily newspaper understands the old adage "No news is good news." The papers are filled with the troubles that plague modern man. Wars, murders, accidents, family tragedies … every day brings a new report of the same old troubles.

Another popular expression synonymous with *trouble* is "the sparks are gonna fly." I remember hearing it quite regularly as a kid: "When your dad gets home, the sparks are gonna fly." There wasn't any doubt in my mind that this spelled trouble. The Old Testament book that specializes in reporting man's troubles is Job. And it is the origin for today's popular phrase.

Biblical Background: Job's troubles were enormous. He was stripped of every material possession as Satan tested his faithfulness to God. He was no stranger to personal tragedy either, as he experienced the loss of his children and was plagued with painful boils from head to toe. Through all this, Job refused to curse God. Eliphas, a personal friend of Job's, paid a visit to "encourage" him. But instead, he actually charged that Job undoubtedly deserved his troubles and pain for some secret sin he was hiding: "Remember, I pray thee, who ever perished, being innocent? or where were the righteous cut off? Even as I have seen, they that plow in iniquity, and sow wickedness, reap the same" (Job 4:7–8).

Eliphas continued to rail against Job, charging that while both foolish and evil men prosper for a time, they are eventually brought to judgment by a righteous God: "Although affliction cometh not forth of the dust, neither doth trouble spring out of the ground; Yet man is born unto trouble, as the sparks fly upward" (Job 5:6–7).

Eliphas was some friend. How would you like your friends coming to your aid and comfort with this line: "Well, friend, all this is all your fault. Now the sparks are gonna fly"? Clearly, Eliphas wasn't the kind of comfort Job required.

Bible Byte: If you've ever sat around a campfire at night, you know that as the embers are stirred, the sparks fly upward. As heated air rises, it lifts the sparks. It is a natural, universal phenomenon. Job's lesson is similar. Man is born unto trouble. It's as natural as the glowing sparks from a fire drifting upward to the heavens, and today's newspapers consistently confirm the pain of man's condition. That condition is sin.

But the old adage "No news is good news" isn't true. For God has good news for man. His son won the victory over sin and the grave, and He ascended into heaven. He intercedes for us with the Father. If we believe in Him, when the Father calls us home, the sparks won't fly but the home fires will be burning brightly.

Straight and Narrow

Matthew 7:13–14

Today's Phrase: As my daughters often remind me, teenagers get it from all sides: There are rules from parents at home and rules from teachers at school. Virtually everywhere they turn, there is an authority figure telling them to mind "the straight and narrow." They certainly know what this phrase implies but probably not where it comes from. Again, Christ's Sermon on the Mount is the source for this age-old directive.

Biblical Background: Christ's mountainside discourse explains that two paths are available to man, two directions from which to choose: "Enter ye in at the strait gate: for wide is the gate, and broad is the way, that leadeth to destruction, and many there be which go in thereat: Because strait is the gate, and narrow is the way, which leadeth unto life, and few there be that find it" (Matthew 7:13–14).

Bible Byte: Years ago, I used to regularly travel to Manhattan for business. Regardless of the time of day, streets were packed with people. One particularly famous street, Broadway, was literally filled with Satan's snares. Openly advertised triple-X movies, pornography, obvious drug influence, and prostitution could be seen everywhere. Considering biblical context, this street was aptly named. It revealed a broad path leading to destruction.

Broad and wide or straight and narrow—the choice is clear. Teens may hear "mind the straight and narrow" more often than they care to; but if they listen, they'll find a path to eternal life. Choosing to ignore God's direction would definitely be a wrong turn.

Seeing Is Believing

John 20:27–28

Today's Phrase: "Hey, I gotta see this for myself!" The phrase "seeing is believing" is very common. We're skeptics by nature, and this phrase confirms that.

An episode in the life of Thomas, one of Jesus's twelve disciples, has generated several lasting and familiar expressions. John 20 relates the events whereby Thomas, familiarly dubbed "Doubting Thomas," gained such colloquial notoriety.

Biblical Background: Following Jesus's resurrection, victory over death was affirmed by His appearance to a small group of disciples gathered in Jerusalem. Thomas was absent. When later he learned of the miracle, Thomas proclaimed a sentiment that serves yet today as the skeptic's rallying cry: "The other disciples therefore said unto him, We have seen the Lord. But he said unto them, Except I shall see in his hands the print of the nails, and put my finger into the print of the nails, and thrust my hand into his side, I will not believe." In other words, "Unless I see for myself, I will not believe" (John 20:25).

"Doubting Thomas" has since evolved into a label synonymous with skepticism and doubt. Actually, the phrase "seeing is believing," is more than a popular expression; it's an accepted philosophy. Yet, while Thomas is remembered for his unbelief, his story doesn't end in doubt.

Eight days after Jesus's original appearance to the disciples, he reappeared.

This time, the group of twelve was complete. Thomas was there too. The Lord invited him to examine the wounds He had suffered on the cross: "Reach hither thy finger, and behold my hands; and reach hither thy hand, and thrust it into my side: and be not faithless, but believing" (John 20:27). Thomas, without hesitation, proclaimed, "My Lord and My God." His doubt was erased, chased, and replaced by a new and confident faith, which Thomas joyously proclaimed.

Jesus teaches, "Blessed are they that have not seen, and yet have believed" (John 20:29). And as Paul reminds us: "For we walk by faith, not by sight" (2 Corinthians 5:7).

Bible Byte: Every day we hear the phrase "seeing is believing." Should we trust only what we see? Let's test the wisdom of that philosophy with a simple test.

Look at the following short phrase and count the number of *f*'s you see:

> Finished files are the result
> of years of scientific study
> combined with the experience
> of many years.

How many *f*'s did you find? Three? Four? Perhaps five? Anyone for six? Look again; the correct answer is six. It's very likely your mind's eye did not "see" the word "of," although it occurs in the sentence three times. Pronounced "o–v," we tend to overlook the obvious *f*'s. This is known as a scotoma, or blind spot. It serves to illustrate a point.

What we see may be real; but what is real, we may not *always* see. Remember, though we may not literally see Christ in the flesh today, He is no less real. It may be tempting to steer by sight, but faith won't steer you wrong.

Saved the Best for Last

John 2:1–11

Today's Phrase: I love chocolate chip cookies. Soft and chewy, moist, and gooey … they're simply my favorite. I have an almost ritualistic eating pattern too. First I like to get rid of the edges, especially if they're a little crisp. Then, I tear the remaining cookie into pieces, eating as I go until all that remains is the buttery, gooey center. That's the absolute best. And I always "save the best for last." Jesus's first New Testament miracle gives us this popular expression. John 2 records the miracle from a wedding feast in Cana.

Biblical Background: Jesus and his disciples were invited guests to the wedding feast, as was Mary, Jesus's mother. Apparently, the bridegroom ran out of wine for his many guests. Sympathetically, Mary told Jesus, "They have no wine." She then directed the servants, "Whatsoever he saith unto you, do it" (John 2:5).

Christ asked the servants to fill six great water pots with water and to serve the water to the governor (or highest-ranking guest) of the feast. The servants did as Christ ordered.

"When the ruler of the feast had tasted the water that was made wine … the governor of the feast called the bridegroom, And saith unto him, Every man at the beginning doth set forth good wine; and when men have well drunk, then that which is worse: but thou hast kept the good wine until now" (John 2:9–10).

In other words, the ruler was amazed the groom had "saved the best for last." Most would have tried to get by with less than the best by passing good wine first, hoping its effect would mask the poorer wine's quality as the feast wore on.

"This beginning of miracles did Jesus in Cana of Galilee, and manifested forth his glory; and his disciples believed in him" (John 2:11).

Bible Byte: The "water to wine" miracle is a rich allegory for a converted sinner. Christ can take a simple empty vessel (our life), fill it with water (His living word), and produce rich and satisfying wine (righteous fruit). We could debate whether the wine was intoxicating or not, but that's not the central issue. What's important is the outcome that can result from spiritual conversion. We might try to pull the wool over people's eyes, and we might get by with it. We might pass for "acceptable wine." But God won't be deceived. He knows us as we truly are. Thankfully, when Christ saves a sinner, the end result is genuinely better. He "saves the best for last." And at the last, for those whom He has converted, eternal life with Him awaits.

See Eye to Eye

Isaiah 52:8

Today's Phrase: Getting two attorneys to agree with one another is an improbable, if not impossible task. Words are always met with more words; debate is met with debate. We term it "legal-ese," a term somewhat irreverently aimed at the overdone complexities of the profession. A lot of folks skeptically believe lawyers *invent* complications. Left to ourselves, we could probably resolve most issues without all the ten-dollar words. In short order, we could "see eye to eye" on the matter. This phrase implies agreement "with one consent." It is expressed in Isaiah 52, and relates not to an argument but to a common joy shared by the children of Israel.

Biblical Background: The prophetic book of Isaiah is not merely an Old Testament work. It is directly quoted in the New Testament over sixty times. Isaiah clearly presents Jesus Christ prophetically. His virgin birth, life, death, resurrection, and second coming are all foretold within the pages of Isaiah. In chapter 52, Isaiah offers a hopeful picture to a captive Jewish nation: "Thy watchmen shall lift up the voice; with the voice together shall they sing: for they shall see eye to eye, when the LORD shall bring again Zion. Break forth into joy, sing together … for the LORD hath comforted his people, he hath redeemed Jerusalem" (Isaiah 52:8–9).

This prophetic word offered genuine hope to the Israelite captives. Yet, while this is a picture of hope, it deals not with a short-term political takeover, as the Israelites may have hoped, but with the coming thousand-year reign of Christ. Still today, many Jews probably do not "see eye to eye" with this interpretation.

Bible Byte: It's probably impossible to agree on everything. We're individuals with our own unique views. Perhaps that's why there are so many different Christian denominations. But one day, with or without attorneys, all believers will sing with one voice, joined in a joyful song of praise at Christ's triumphant return.

No one knows exactly when that will occur, but let's not argue. He will come again. And when He comes, every living soul will know and agree *He* is Lord. At that time, at that instant, all mankind will "see eye to eye." For some, the song won't be so joyful. What song will you be singing?

Stand and Face the Music

Daniel 3:5

Today's Phrase: Life offers many choices. Some are simple; others are very difficult; but all have consequences. The consequences may be immediate or long-term. We may stumble into them unaware or boldly face a known outcome. Meeting and accepting the known, unavoidable consequences of our choices is familiarly expressed, "stand and face the music."

A fascinating episode during the reign of King Nebuchadnezzar is the likely origin for the expression "stand and face the music." Several differing opinions exist regarding its origin, however. Some suggest that it comes from the 1930s Irving Berlin song "Let's Face the Music and Dance." Another suggests it relates to a nervous actor facing a large audience across the open orchestra pit. Others believe it stems from the former practice of "drumming" a dishonored soldier out of the military. Again, let's examine a possible biblical derivation.

Biblical Background: Daniel 3 opens with King Nebuchadnezzar's decree for construction of an enormous golden image on the vast plains of Babylon. During the dedication ceremony, the king commands that all are to worship the idol whenever they "hear the sound of the cornet, flute, harp, sackbut, psaltery, dulcimer, and all kinds of musick" (Daniel 3:5). As the king's musicians played, loyal subjects everywhere within the kingdom would fall down to worship this golden image. Those risking refusal faced certain death.

Three young Jewish men took that risk. It did not take long for ambitious political informants to report Shadrach, Meshach, and Abednego to an incredulous King Nebuchadnezzar. The story is well known. The king allowed the three a chance to change their minds, but they insistently refused to bow down to worship a false god. King Nebuchadnezzar furiously ordered them bound and cast into a fiery furnace.

The intense heat and flames consumed several of the executioners as guards placed the three within the flaming furnace. But, as Shadrach, Meshach, and Abednego had boldly proclaimed, the true God spared them without a single hair of their heads being singed (Daniel 3:27).

Nebuchadnezzar, witness to this miracle, reacted swiftly. Not only did he promote the three within the provincial government of Babylon, but also he further decreed it unlawful to "speak any thing amiss against [their] God" (Daniel 3:29). Clearly, he changed his tune.

Bible Byte: Shadrach, Meshach, and Abednego made a difficult choice. At a time when most were willing to blindly follow the crowd and the king's decree, these three steadfastly refused to worship a false god. They stood bravely for the cause of faith, and by refusing to bow down, they willingly, and quite literally, "stood and faced the music."

Long ago someone said, "If you don't stand for something, you may fall for anything." Life's difficult choices won't ever be totally eliminated, but standing with God can certainly make sweeter music of the consequences.

Scapegoat

Leviticus 16:7–10, 21–22

Today's Phrase: Competition in business can be fierce. And sometimes, competition to get a jump on coworkers is even more ruthless. I've never had much appetite for it, but I've certainly seen my share of its effects. To some, getting ahead is the most important part of any job. They maneuver, manipulate, and malign; they do anything to look good. If something goes sour with a program or plan they're involved with, they immediately begin to look for a "scapegoat," someone to take the fall, endure the shame, and accept the blame. With a suitable "scapegoat," their own records remain spotless. Ancient temple ritual gives us the term "scapegoat," and surprisingly, it is used in a remarkably similar way.

Biblical Background: The Day of Atonement was an extremely important day in Jewish temple worship. Marked by meticulous preparations inside and outside the temple, this day was unique in its ritual of sacrifice and atonement for sin.

The chief priest was to find two goats from the livestock. One goat would be sacrificed on the temple altar to the Lord; the other goat would "be presented alive before the LORD, to make an atonement with him, and to let him go for a scapegoat into the wilderness" (Leviticus 16:10). Following the blood sacrifice of the Lord's goat, the chief priest dealt with the remaining animal.

"And Aaron shall lay both his hands upon the head of the live goat, and confess over him all the iniquities of the children of Israel, and all their transgressions in all their sins, putting them upon the head of the goat, and shall send him away by the hand of a fit man into the wilderness: And the goat shall bear upon him all their iniquities unto a land not inhabited: and he shall let go the goat in the wilderness" (Leviticus 16:21–22).

Bible Byte: A "scapegoat" takes the guilt and shame for others. In an example such as everyday business, often it's subordinates, people unable to speak out to defend themselves. In ancient Jewish ritual, it was simply an innocent animal. Banished to the wilderness, it bore the inequity of Israel's sin.

The scapegoat is a beautiful picture of Christ. He, too, undeservedly bore the guilt and sin of us all. And He took it in silence, willingly suffering the shame. He bore our sins on Calvary's cross, so that our guilt and shame would be forever removed from us. Thanks to Him, our record is clean. We don't have to take the fall. And we don't have to look far to find Him. In fact, He's looking for you.

Stinks to High Heaven

Leviticus 1:9, 13, 17; 2:2

Today's Phrase: Not long ago, many people in my work area became annoyed with a rather persistent and quite offensive odor. "Something around here stinks to high heaven," I remember one coworker stated, "and we've got to find it!" You may have guessed it was a mouse, quite dead and hidden away behind a file cabinet. The phrase "stinks to high heaven" more than aptly described its offensive smell of decay.

As strange as it seems, this phrase is derived from scripture. It relates to the ancient religious sacrifices and burnt offerings described in the Old Testament. The book of Leviticus is more than likely the basis for today's expression.

Biblical Background: Leviticus details many religious rituals observed by the Jewish people. Each sacrifice had a specific purpose, and many actually symbolically portray Christ's sacrificial death. The burnt offering is perhaps the oldest sacrifice known to man. There are many biblical references to animal sacrifice and burnt offerings, many more than the few I've listed from Leviticus. Examples from well-known Genesis stories include offerings of Abraham, Noah, and Abel. In each case, as in these verses from Leviticus, the ritual included these words: "And burn it upon the altar; it is a burnt sacrifice, an offering made by fire, of a sweet savour unto the LORD" (Leviticus 1:9, 13, 17; 2:2).

The burnt offering was completely consumed in fire. Only the ashes remained. The Hebrew name for this rite of sacrifice is *Olah*, which means "that which ascends." Literally, the smoke rising to the heavens was "a sweet savour unto the Lord."

The Jews used specific animals from their flocks and herds. Wild or hunted animals were forbidden. Clearly, mild and meek domesticated animals are much more representative of Christ than a wild, carnivorous beast. Similarly, animals were to be made clean and unspotted. Finally, the offering must be a willing gift. When these conditions were met, the sacrifice was acceptable and pleasing to God. If not, the sacrifice was not acceptable. An acceptable sacrifice was a sweet-smelling savour; it follows that an unacceptable sacrifice would have stunk to high heaven.

Bible Byte: Christ is the picture of a pleasing, perfect sacrifice: male, without blemish, meek yet strong, and offered willingly by a loving God. His sacrificial death put an end to the ongoing need for blood atonement for sins. As stated before, He died "once and for all." If we accept that, believe in Him, and turn from our sins, we will not end this life in rot and decay but rather with the hope and promise of life eternal. Without Christ, life goes up in smoke, and just like death, it stinks to high heaven.

Set Your House in Order

2 Kings 20:1
Isaiah 38:1

Today's Phrase: There's been a great deal of emphasis in recent years on prearranged funeral details, estate planning, and wills. As an "organization nut," the concept appeals to my need for order. But, at this point, all I've managed to check off that list is a will. I've had many lunchroom conversations about these topics. Quite frequently, someone will say, "I know I need to *set my house in order*, but I'm too busy living to plan my dying." Another friend quotes an old John Lennon song: "Life is what happens when you're busy making plans."

Well, those rationalizations may be popular and sound clever; but the admonition to "set your house in order" is not a new one. The Old Testament originates the expression in Isaiah's prophetic charge to a dying King Hezekiah.

Biblical Background: "In those days was Hezekiah sick unto death. And Isaiah the prophet the son of Amoz came unto him, and said unto him, Thus saith the LORD, Set thine house in order: for thou shalt die, and not live" (Isaiah 38:1; 2 Kings 20:1).

Bible Byte: Hezekiah, a good king, did not ignore the advice. But he didn't call his lawyer or the funeral home or his financial planner. He called upon the Lord: "Then Hezekiah turned his face toward the wall, and prayed unto the LORD" (Isaiah 38:2).

How about you? Have you called upon the Lord to "set your house in order?" You must make a choice. Make that choice before it's too late. "As for me and my house, we will serve the LORD" (Joshua 24:15).

Spittin' Image

Genesis 1:27
Genesis 2:7

Today's Phrase: With five children, it's been fun to hear people liken each one to my wife or me or some distant descendant—"Bobby sure looks like you," or "Boy, he sure looks a lot like Gail."

We've all seen children who are near mirror reflections of one parent or another. Facial features, a smile, and even mannerisms give them away. We might say, "He's the *spittin' image* of his father." Does this strange phrase originate from scripture too? You bet. Helped along by a slight Southern drawl, this phrase has evolved right from the pages of Genesis.

Biblical Background: The creation story is a remarkable tale. The wonders of this earth, of the universe, spoken into existence by the word of God are incredible. While some may choose to believe man evolved from a blob or a single-celled organism, Genesis states otherwise: "So God created man in his own image, in the image of God created he him; male and female created he them" (Genesis 1:27). "And the LORD God formed man of the dust of the ground, and breathed into his nostrils the breath of life; and man became a living soul" (Genesis 2:7).

God created man in His own image. God also gave man a spirit. Spirit and image—do you see the connection yet? If a child looks like his father, in his image, and has a similar temperament, a similar spirit, it might be said he was made in the "spirit and image" of his father. Add a little playful Southern accent and you get "spirit n' image." Spoken lazily, the phrase sounds like "spittin' image." Some sources agree this phrase is very likely an African American slang expression derived from the Genesis account of man's creation in "the spirit and image" of God, the Father.

Bible Byte: When I was a kid, most folks said I looked like my mother. That's not at all bad. But, today, I'd rather people be reminded of my Father, my *heavenly* Father, that is. When someone sees you, can they see the *spirit and image* of your heavenly Father? We can never achieve perfection, but hopefully, we can mirror Christ's love for others. We must strive to be His "spittin' image."

Safety in Numbers

Proverbs 11:14

Today's Phrase: My daughters are too rapidly approaching the dating years, and I, for one, am not all eager. Fortunately, there's a growing trend toward large group dates. Psychologists say these are great to reduce peer pressure. For me, I simply say there's generally "safety in numbers." This old expression is aptly found in the ageless wisdom of Proverbs.

Biblical Background: Someone once said that a proverb is a short sentence drawn from long experience. In scripture, Solomon, the son of David and king of Israel, authored the book of Proverbs. There are many wonderful sayings contained in its pages. The phrase "safety in numbers" is one of them. "Where no counsel is, the people fall: but in the multitude of counselors there is safety" (Proverbs 11:14).

Bible Byte: Safety in numbers is short and sweet counsel ... a short sentence drawn from long experience. When we try to go our own way, when we only listen to ourselves, we listen to a fool. There is "safety in numbers." And as my daughters start to date in a few years, I'll hope to make sure the number is greater than two.

Salt of the Earth

Matthew 5:13

Today's Phrase: Some people have a certain way about them that everybody likes: pleasant, always smiling, and a kind word or helping hand for anybody. Bring up this person's name in a crowd, and you'll get an immediate reaction. "Great guy" or "super gal" some might say. It's also common to hear reference to a rather strange expression: "He's the salt of the earth."

Since salt has a slightly bitter taste, what is it about the origin of this phrase that implies goodness? Let's look to Christ's Sermon on the Mount to see.

Biblical Background: Matthew 5 begins Christ's Sermon on the Mount. Teaching His disciples, Jesus says, "Ye are the salt of the earth: but if the salt have lost his savour, wherewith shall it be salted? it is thenceforth good for nothing, but to be cast out, and to be trodden under foot of men" (Matthew 5:13).

In ancient times, with no refrigeration, salt was used to preserve foods. The meat was covered with salt, which prevented, or least delayed, spoiling from bacteria.

Jesus's expression was a colorful analogy to His followers. They, no doubt, understood their role to preserve the world from sin's evil decay. And, if salt could no longer preserve and protect, it was good for nothing except to be cast out to the ground and trampled underfoot.

Bible Byte: We, as Christians, are called to be the "salt of the earth," not to make everyone like us but to preserve and protect those we meet from the rot and decay of sin's evil grip. How do we accomplish that? Through telling others about Christ and by living a Christian life of kindness and service to others. Christians are called to be salt and light in the world. And, if we lose our ability or courage, to preserve Christ in the world, our service to others, no matter how much they might like us, is good for nothing.

Sign of the Times

Matthew 16:3

Today's Phrase: As mild breezes and the warmth of the sun greeted us this spring, it didn't take long for an enterprising youngster to hit the streets with a lemonade stand. A local newspaper published a photo of the bustling business with its little entrepreneur, her paper cups and pitcher, and her cardboard sign advertising "Lemonade—5 Cents." The news photo carried the caption "Sign of the Times." It humored me to know the liberal press quoted the Bible. That's right. The phrase "sign of the times" is an exact phrase appearing in Matthew's gospel record.

Biblical Background: The Pharisees and Sadducees, religious sects of the day, were always eager to tempt Jesus into proving His authority and His ministry. In Matthew 16, a crowd of Jews from these sects challenged Christ to "shew them a sign from heaven."

"He answered and said unto them, When it is evening, ye say, It will be fair weather: for the sky is red. And in the morning, It will be foul weather to day: for the sky is red and lowering. O ye hypocrites, ye can discern the face of the sky; but can ye not discern the signs of the times?" (Matthew 16:2–3)

Jesus met their challenge with a challenge of His own. These men were educated, well-read in the ancient scriptures. They even understood the signs of the weather.

But they missed a sign given from the Old Testament. "Therefore the

Lord himself shall give you a sign; Behold, a virgin shall conceive, and bear a son, and shall call his name Immanuel" (Isaiah 7:14). In Christ Jesus, this prophetic sign was fulfilled. Before them stood a "sign of the times," but they missed the signal.

Bible Byte: The newspaper caption was most appropriate. The signs of spring and warm summer days ahead were reflected in that little girl's lemonade stand. And as we consider the world we live in, there are also many other signs, equally evident and equally accurate. The times of our day are an amazing fulfillment of many Bible prophecies. We're living right in the midst of it, and yet some fail to see the signs. How about you? Don't ignore the "signs of the times." Trade your newspaper for a Bible and start checking the signals.

SKIN OF MY TEETH

Job 19:20

Today's Phrase: In a large family, budgeting can get to be more art than science. There always seems to be some unexpected expense that hits at the wrong time. I suppose there never really is a right time, but some months I just make it. I get by just by the "skin of my teeth." The implication is a "narrow escape," but actually and thankfully, the Lord always provides.

The Old Testament book of Job is the origin for today's expression. It, too, deals with a narrow escape, but it also shows the overwhelming abundance of blessing available from God Almighty.

Biblical Background: Job is an interesting book. It presents the account of a good and righteous man, Job. It's a story of suffering, of Job's abundance, decline, and ultimate restoration. It's a fascinating example of a faithful man's view of the blessings and disappointments delivered by life and, at the very least, teaches us to make pearls out of life's irritations.

Job was a wealthy man, rich in family, land, cattle, and possessions. Yet, he was faithful to God and led a very spiritual life marked by close fellowship with God. The early chapters of Job set the stage for this drama. Satan challenges Job's righteousness. Satan claims that Job's faith would change if he lost his good fortune. God permits Satan to strip Job's wealth, destroying all that he has. Still, Job refuses to curse

God. Satan then accuses, since Job isn't personally or physically harmed, he can easily remain faithful, and if Satan were allowed to harm Job, his faith would waiver and he would then renounce his faith in God.

Again, the Lord permits Satan to do what he willed, but Job's life is to be spared. The account of Job's maladies is tortuous. From an emotional loss of his entire family to an affliction of festering boils head to toe, Job is fiendishly attacked. His wife wails, "Curse God and die!" Even his friends suggest Job should repent, thinking some secret sin must have merited such horrible judgment. Job still refuses to renounce God. He doesn't understand, but he remains faithful. In Chapter 19, Job laments, "All my inward friends abhorred me: and they whom I loved are turned against me. My bone cleaveth to my skin and to my flesh, and I am escaped with the skin of my teeth" (Job 19:19–20).

Job's faithfulness never wavered. While he was never sure of the reasons for his suffering, he accepted it, endured it, and was ultimately restored to full mercy and blessings from God: "So the LORD blessed the latter end of Job more than his beginning" (Job 42:12).

Bible Byte: Yes, sometimes we do just barely get by. But God is faithful. He provides. And, I admit, He indulges me far beyond my needs. (Truthfully, my wants are responsible for the stretch in my budget.) Still, He's patient with me. And, hopefully, I'll find my eternal rest with Him in heaven. Certainly, my latter end would be greater than my beginning. I'll put up with a few narrow escapes here on earth, as long as I escape the snares of hell, even if only "by the skin of my teeth."

Sweat Blood

Luke 22:44

Today's Phrase: A situation involving my oldest daughter recently reminded me of the phrase "sweat blood." She had tried out for cheerleading, along with two dozen other eager girls, and on this particular day was anxiously awaiting the outcome of the selection vote. She paced. She nervously thumped. She prayed. She rationalized. Her anticipation was intense. She wanted it so badly. She was really "sweating blood."

This figurative expression implies great anxiety and intensity. It originates from the ancient scriptural writings of those who were eyewitnesses to Christ's sufferings.

Biblical Background: Just prior to His capture at the hands of Judas in the Garden of Gethsemane, Jesus knelt to pray, "Father, if thou be willing, remove this cup from me: nevertheless not my will, but thine, be done" (Luke 22:42). We must remember that while Christ was God in the flesh, He was also a man. His anguish was great as He knowingly recognized the cruel death He would soon face.

"And there appeared an angel unto him from heaven, strengthening him. And being in an agony he prayed more earnestly: and his sweat was as it were great drops of blood falling down to the ground" (Luke 22:43–44).

Clearly, Jesus agonized over the outcome. He said, in effect, "Take this bitter end from me, Father, if we can accomplish it any other way. But, if it is your will that I should face it, of course, I will obey." Though Christ "sweat blood" over the outcome, He was willing to submit His own will to that of His Father's.

Bible Byte: To "sweat blood" reflects the intensity and anxiety of our will. When we want a particular event to turn out just as we will it, our agonizing is reflected in this expression. Christ, too, agonized over what He knew He would face upon Calvary's cross. As a man, He didn't want to face it. But He earnestly prayed to the point of "sweating blood" and submitted to the will of His Father. In doing so, He willingly went to His death. And, His *shed blood* covers our sins. Thanks to His sacrifice, we don't have to sweat blood about the outcome of our lives. If we believe in Him, the outcome will turn out perfectly, just as it did, by the way, for my cheerleading daughter.

Send a Boy to Do a Man's Job

1 Samuel 17:33

Today's Phrase: The phrase "send a boy to do a man's job," conjures up a strong personal recollection. I remember as if yesterday, my first morning aboard ship as a twenty-two-year-old, baby-faced, wet-behind-the-ears naval officer. I was a mere one-stripe ensign, standing before a salty crew of forty-five enlisted men. I felt like a hamburger before a pack of hungry hounds. Fortunately, I knew enough to value their professionalism and experience. I relied heavily upon it. In other words, I hit the deck listening to others, not barking at orders. In a short while, I earned both the experience I lacked and the respect I desired. But I clearly remember their expressions and their eyes that day. Each disgustedly said, "Uncle Sam sent us another boy to do a man's job."

Biblical Background: The popular children's story of David and Goliath is the basis for this expression. The warring Philistines were on one mountain and the nation of Israel platooned on another. A great valley separated them, but they were both set to do battle. Out of the Philistine camp came Goliath, a towering giant of a man and obviously a mighty warrior. The first book of Samuel, chapter 17, states he stood to a height of "six cubits and a span." (A cubit is 21.8 inches, while estimates for a span are about 9 inches. This places Goliath at over 11.5 feet.) Goliath cried out across the valley with a challenge. Paraphrased, his challenge was "I am one man, a Philistine. Let's not have our entire armies battle. Let your side choose a man among you and we alone shall determine the victor."

"And the Philistine said, I defy the armies of Israel this day; give me a man, that we might fight together" (1 Samuel 17:10).

Goliath taunted the Israelites for forty days with this challenge, and clearly, King Saul and all the men of Israel were afraid, all, that is, but young David. This young shepherd boy, youngest of the sons of Jesse, appealed to Saul to be allowed to do battle with the giant. Saul understandably chided him.

"Thou art not able to go against this Philistine to fight with him: for thou art but a youth, and he a man of war from his youth" (1 Samuel 17:33).

Saul says, in effect, "I can't send a boy to do a man's job." But David persists, citing the confidence he has in the Lord of Israel. Saul reluctantly relents, saying, "Go, and the LORD be with thee" (1 Samuel 17:37).

The rest of the story is well known. David scorned the armor of Saul and took only five smooth stones and a sling. But these would prove sufficient. As he stands before the giant, David is met with disgust. "And when the Philistine looked about, and saw David, he disdained him: for he was but a youth, and ruddy, and of fair countenance" (1 Samuel 17:42). Yet this baby-faced youth with his faith in God, slew the great Goliath. With but one small shot from his sling, Goliath was toppled.

Bible Byte: Reflecting back, on my first day aboard ship, my confidence was shaken. But when young David stood before a much more imposing foe, he was steadfast and sure. I was lucky. I put my trust in others, and eventually earned their trust in return. David put his faith and his life in God's hands. God was faithful, and David prevailed.

The Bible teaches we should accept God with the innocence and trust of childlike faith. We don't need to be a mighty warrior or a strong man. Christ already fought the battle and won. We need only believe in Christ. Permit me to continue the military analogy as I borrow a very familiar United States Marine Corps recruiting slogan. God is "looking for a few good men," but all they need is the faith of a child.

Toss Him to the Lions

Daniel 6:16–17

Today's Phrase: "Oh, let him fend for himself. Toss him to the lions." This popular phrase implies abandonment and comes from a very familiar story from Daniel 6 in the Old Testament.

Biblical Background: Darius was the new king of the conquered Babylonian empire. He had recently led the Medes in the march against Babylon and now sat on the palace throne. Darius established one hundred and twenty princes and three presidents over his empire. Daniel, of the tribe of Judah, was the first president, or prime minister. He was also Darius's favorite.

Darius's other appointees were jealous of Daniel. They watched him closely, waiting to capitalize on any fault or breach of loyalty he might display toward the king. But they could find none, for Daniel was faithful and God-fearing. Realizing he would not betray his loyalty, the other princes knew they must trap Daniel in a contradiction between his faithful service to Darius and his commitment of faith to God.

Their scheme was to persuade King Darius to sign a decree that no man could ask a petition of *any* god, only of Darius himself, for a period of thirty days. Failure to comply would mean death in the lion's den. When word of the ruling came to Daniel, he chose to serve God rather than some ill-advised, man-made decree. He went about his normal prayer life, making petitions to God in prayer three times a day. The trap had been set, as Daniel prayed, and Daniel's enemies now eagerly preyed upon him.

Daniel was soon discovered. Darius regretted his statute as soon as he realized Daniel had violated it. Yet, the law could not be changed. Daniel had to be thrown into the lion's den. As Darius issued the command to toss Daniel to the lions, he said to him, "Thy God whom thou servest continually, he will deliver thee" (Daniel 6:16). Then, the den was sealed with a huge stone, and Daniel was left inside to die.

The next morning, King Darius rose early and quickly went to the den of lions. "And when he came to the den, he cried with a lamentable voice ... O Daniel, servant of the living God, is thy God, whom thou servest continually, able to deliver thee from the lions?" (Daniel 6:20).

Daniel lived, and he answered King Darius, "My God hath sent his angel, and hath shut the lions' mouths, that they have not hurt me" (Daniel 6:22).

Bible Byte: There are times when all of us feel alone, abandoned by our friends, left to fend for ourselves. But we're never alone if we have God. Daniel had been abandoned but was still surrounded by God Almighty. He had been kept safe in the midst of danger. We might never face a den filled with dangerous animals, but there is a lion that's out of his cage and always looking for fresh prey. "Be sober, be vigilant; because your adversary the devil, as a roaring lion, walketh about, seeking whom he may devour" (1 Peter 5:8). Surrounded by God's love, we never have to face that dreadful roar alone.

Thorn in My Side

2 Corinthians 12:7

Today's Phrase: No matter what business you're in, there's an unwritten rule of the trade: "The customer is always right." That's a great philosophy for business, but boy, can it test your patience. Some people can be terribly demanding, rude, and inconsiderate. Customers or not, they're genuine pains. They certainly earn the label "thorn in my side."

Biblical Background: This expression is most likely derived from Paul's second letter to the Corinthian church. Paul, too, had a "thorn in the flesh." But he dealt with it a little more graciously than most: "There was given to me a thorn in the flesh, the messenger of Satan to buffet me, lest I should be exalted above measure. For this thing I besought the Lord thrice, that it might depart from me" (2 Corinthians 12:7–8).

Paul's humanity is reflected in his repeated appeals to the Lord. Three times he asked God to remove his "thorn in the flesh." But Paul is answered contrary to his wishes.

"And he said unto me, My grace is sufficient for thee: for my strength is made perfect in weakness" (2 Corinthians 12:9).

Paul's reaction is remarkable. He doesn't pout. He doesn't complain. He doesn't silently endure either. Instead, he rejoices: "Most gladly therefore will I rather glory in my infirmities, that the power of Christ may rest upon me. Therefore I take pleasure in infirmities, in reproaches, in necessities, in persecutions, in distresses for Christ's sake: for when I am weak, then I am strong" (2 Corinthians 12:9–10).

Bible Byte: Paul is not only a model of patience but also a model of attitude. He recognized his weakness was an opportunity for God to display his strength. Paul's desire for dependence and fellowship with God outweighed his desire for personal comfort. In effect he says, "I'm happy in my human weakness, for God becomes more real to me as I rest in His strength."

We're never told what Paul's "thorn" is. I don't think that's an accident. As a result, everyone can relate to Paul's condition, for the "thorn" could be anything. Paul confirms that God's grace is an ointment to soothe the sting from *any* thorn, including Satan's darts. And the devil is a mighty tough customer.

Took Me under His Wing

Matthew 23:37
Psalm 91:4–5

Today's Phrase: I once worked with a large corporation as a field representative based in Los Angeles. With just over one year's experience under my belt, I wasn't very technically prepared. I must admit I wasn't truly ready for such a demanding job in a large metropolitan market. Fortunately, one of my major clients was an older gentleman in his sixties. He was seasoned, experienced, and understanding and an excellent teacher. I was a willing student. He "took me under his wing," and as a result, I not only survived the experience; I thrived. Whenever I hear the phrase "took me under his wing," I remember Mr. Jim Miller. I also remember those scriptural passages that are the basis for today's popular expression.

Biblical Background: In a red-letter edition of the Bible, the words actually spoken by Christ are highlighted in red. Matthew 23 is virtually completely red. In this discourse, Jesus speaks to the multitude on three subjects: He warns the people about the hypocrisy of scribes and Pharisees, He denounces the sin of pride and feigned religion reflected in their actions, and He weeps over the people of Jerusalem who reject Him. You can sense the love and anguish Christ felt for the people as he proclaimed, "O Jerusalem, Jerusalem, thou that killest the prophets, and stonest them which are sent unto thee, how often would I have gathered thy children together, even as a hen gathereth her chickens under her wings, and ye would not!" (Matthew 23:37).

In the Old Testament book of Psalms, yet another clear picture is given reflecting this phrase and the protection it implies: "He shall cover thee with his feathers, and under his wings shalt thou trust: his truth shall be thy shield and buckler. Thou shalt not be afraid for the terror by night; nor for the arrow that flieth by day" (Psalm 91:4–5).

Bible Byte: I once heard of a terrible barn fire, which destroyed most animals on the farm. As the farmer kicked around in the ashes the next day, his boot disturbed a blackened heap in one corner of the barn. At once, several chicks scurried away from under their charred mother hen. Christ is a picture of that depth of care and protection. He gave His life for you and me, so that in His death, we can be safe, safe from the fires of hell. He wants to take you "under His wing." Don't turn away. Take refuge under His wings and thrive.

Turn the Other Cheek

Matthew 5:39

Today's Phrase: Christmas shopping amidst the Christmas rush can be maddening. The joy of the season is wonderful, but the mall parking lots can be battlefields. Last year, I remember circling the lot for what seemed like hours, though it was actually more like thirty minutes. Finally, I eyed my spot. Unfortunately, so did someone in a sleek and fast little Honda. Before I could get there, and in spite of my mental stake on the territory, I was beaten out by that little black car. My mind said, "Don't get mad. Get even!" But thankfully, my wife reminded me, "Turn the other cheek, honey." She was right. Though frustrated, I tried to chuckle and kept searching.

Biblical Background: The Sermon on the Mount is the source for this popular expression.

"Ye have heard that it hath been said, An eye for an eye, and a tooth for a tooth: But I say unto you, That ye resist not evil: but whosoever shall smite thee on thy right cheek, turn to him the other also" (Matthew 5:38–39).

Bible Byte: The biblical mandate to "turn the other cheek" certainly doesn't play well by modern standards. In today's world, it seems we are out for ourselves. As the saying goes, "It's a dog-eat-dog world." But a slap on the cheek can sometimes be a blessing. When you "turn the other cheek," you might see things more clearly. (Just as I did that day, when I eventually saw another parking spot about ten rows closer to the mall.)

Time and Place for Everything

Ecclesiastes 3:1

Today Phrase: As a youngster, I truly enjoyed rock music. I played in several bands, which my parents patiently tolerated, but I know they never fully appreciated the lyrics from any of the popular songs we played. (Most often I remember them complaining they couldn't even *hear* the lyrics through all our racket.)

Still, I felt the rockers of my youth were genuine "visionaries"; the prophets for our time; the philosophers, poets, and messengers of a new wisdom. One of my favorite songs was "Turn! Turn! Turn!" by the Byrds. I felt it was "inspired." The song's lyrics included this verse:

> To everything (Turn! Turn! Turn!)
> There is a season (Turn! Turn! Turn!)
> And a time to every purpose under heaven.

In my mind, that was a beautifully poetic expression confirming the phrase "there's a time and place for everything." Not until I became a Christian years later did I discover these lyrics actually were inspired. They are contained in Solomon's Old Testament writing in the book of Ecclesiastes.

Biblical Background: The third chapter of Ecclesiastes presents one of several philosophies Solomon pursued in his quest for satisfaction and fulfillment apart from God. It's a viewpoint that suggests that "fate" controls life, "whatever will be, will be." The Byrds must have subscribed to it, for their lyrics are almost verbatim from Solomon's test.

"To every thing there is a season, and a time to every purpose under the heaven: A time to be born, and a time to die; a time to plant, and a time to pluck up that which is planted; A time to kill, and a time to heal; a time to break down, and a time to build up; A time to weep, and a time to laugh; a time to mourn, and a time to dance; A time to cast away stones, and a time to gather stones together; a time to embrace, and a time to refrain from embracing; A time to get, and a time to lose; a time to keep, and a time to cast away; A time to rend, and a time to sew; a time to keep silence, and a time to speak; A time to love, and a time to hate; a time of war, and a time of peace" (Ecclesiastes 3:1–8).

Clearly, if taken out of context, this passage does, in fact, state, "there's a time, a place for everything; whatever will be, will be." But there's great danger in using isolated passages from scripture to draw broad conclusions.

Ecclesiastes is often quoted out of context and is a favorite of various cults and atheists. That sounds shocking, but not when you understand the context in which Ecclesiastes was written. Solomon received godly wisdom, but he foolishly tried every pursuit of pleasure and philosophy known to man. He wanted to find fulfillment and satisfaction apart from God. Ecclesiastes is the summary of his experiences. Taken out of context, Ecclesiastes can "justify" almost anything. But Solomon concludes the pursuit is foolishness. He concludes that the world's pleasures and philosophies are "vanity," "nothingness," or "emptiness." He ultimately recognized that man cannot be satisfied apart from God. And that's the ultimate conclusion missing from most quotes taken out of context from this important book.

Bible Byte: I'm not sorry I had the experience of playing in rock bands in my youth. As I look back, it was a growth period. And, I suppose, it was an appropriate "time and place" for the idealism of my youth. But I'm thankful God led me to a more solid foundation than the philosophers of the rock world. He led me to the true rock, His Son, Jesus Christ. How about you? There's no better time or place to turn toward God. Turn! Turn! Turn!

Thick Skinned

1 Kings 12:10

Today's Phrase: My oldest daughter has a very sweet, sensitive spirit. She has a real heart for the less fortunate, and one day I'm sure the good Lord will use her talents. But her sensitivities can be a liability as well. She wears her heart on her sleeve and is easily hurt. In other words, she's not very "thick skinned." A "thick-skinned" person accepts criticism well and is callous to the hardships or tragedies of others. Rehoboam, the son of Solomon, provides an ancient model for the modern implication of today's expression "thick skinned."

Biblical Background: Chapter 11 of 1 Kings concludes with Solomon's death and his son Rehoboam's assumption to the throne of Israel. In short order, the people of Israel approached their new king to request a reduction in taxes: "And all the congregation of Israel came, and spake unto Rehoboam, saying, Thy father made our yoke grievous: now therefore make thou the grievous service of thy father, and his heavy yoke which he put upon us, lighter, and we will serve thee" (1 Kings 12:3–4).

Rehoboam considered their request, inviting their return in three days' time for his decision. In the meantime, he sought the counsel of his father's wise men. They suggested he consent to the people's wishes, for he could earn their loyalty and service forever through that simple act. Yet, Rehoboam sought a second opinion. He went to several young men, friends he had grown up with. Their advice was different: "And the young men that were grown up with him spake unto him, saying, Thus shalt thou speak unto this people … My little finger shall be thicker than my father's loins. And now whereas my father did lade you with a heavy yoke, I will add to your yoke: my father hath chastised you with whips, but I will chastise you with scorpions" (1 Kings 12:10–11).

Unfortunately, Rehoboam chose to follow this advice. He dealt insensitively with his people and their burden. Ultimately, ten northern tribes rebelled and split the kingdom. Rehoboam's lack of compassion and "thick skin" divided the nation of Israel.

Bible Byte: Being insensitive to the needs of others always creates division, whether it is a kingdom, as in Rehoboam's day; a workplace; or a home. Putting the needs and concerns of others above your own requires sacrificial love. Consider Christ as He hung on the cross. He thought not of himself but of the sinners He would die for. Was He "thick skinned"? No, not at all. He had a heart for people, God's heart. And He selflessly gave it for us. Don't be "thick skinned," but more importantly, don't be "thick headed." Accept Christ today.

Turned the Tables

John 2:15

Today's Phrase: A recent headline in the sports section read, "Cubs Turn the Tables on Cards." It was a clever play on words since references suggest the phrase relates to casino card games. Today, it implies a change of luck; but a Bible verse in John suggests this expression dates back to a much more ancient "turn of the tables."

Biblical Background: Shortly before His betrayal and crucifixion, Jesus entered Jerusalem at the Passover feast, riding upon a young donkey. He drew great crowds of people; but while many of the people praised Him and threw palm branches at His feet, many did not know Him. He must have shocked the multitude when He dismounted and immediately charged into the temple.

"And (Jesus) found in the temple those that sold oxen and sheep and doves, and the changers of money sitting: And when he had made a scourge of small cords, he drove them all out of the temple, and the sheep, and the oxen; and poured out the changers' money, and overthrew the tables" (John 2:14–15).

Christ was clearly angry. The Jews had corrupted the temple by profiting from the exchange of Roman coins for Jewish coins and by selling animals for sacrifice. This business cheapened both the temple and their worship. Matthew's gospel account of this event states, "It is written,

My house shall be called the house of prayer; but ye have made it a den of thieves" (Matthew 21:13).

Bible Byte: Today's phrase has come to colloquially express a change of events from win to lose, from good luck to bad luck. Christ "turned the tables" on religious hypocrisy. His act did not symbolize a change of luck but rather the need for a change of heart. Consider your heart today. If it isn't right with God, invite Christ to "turn the tables."

Ten Times Better

Daniel 1:20

Today's Phrase: Living in an old house requires a "jack of all trades." I've not mastered any, of course, but I've tried, out of necessity, a little plumbing, carpentry, painting, electrical work, and more. I'm never quite sure of myself, but after any fix-up projects, I check with my wife. If she says, "That works ten times better," then I know I've done okay. Surprisingly, this expression is found in Daniel.

Biblical Background: Following Nebuchadnezzar's siege of Jerusalem, certain of the children of Israel were taken captive into the king's palace. These were considered the brightest and fairest, and were to be taught the knowledge and tongue of their captors, the Chaldeans. Daniel was among this select group of prisoners.

Nebuchadnezzar established not only a special educational diet but a special physical diet as well. But Daniel, being Jewish, could not eat certain animals considered unclean by his religious traditions. He chose to refuse the king's established menu of meats and wines, and instead had a simple grain diet and water. Melzar, the guard in charge of these special prisoners, was worried that Daniel and others who refused the king's provisions would soon turn weak and pale. Yet Daniel persuaded Melzar to permit them to abstain from the king's menu for ten days. After the test, Daniel and his friends appeared fairer and fatter than those on the king's diet. Amazed, Melzar now permitted Daniel to continue, allowing him to remain true to his faith.

Daniel's obedience was rewarded by God, who "gave them knowledge and skill in all learning and wisdom: and Daniel had understanding in all visions and dreams" (Daniel 1:17). Nebuchadnezzar was amazed at his wisdom and understanding. "He found them ten times better than all the magicians and astrologers that were in all his realm" (Daniel 1:20).

Bible Byte: God's care and nurture of these captives provides a rich illustration of contrasts. Just as the king's provisions appeared to be superior, the world's menu can be very appealing. But the diet chosen by Daniel was one of faithful submission. While it might appear bland, it is far better, ten times better, than that offered by the world. The table is set, and there are two selections: a diet fit for a king or one from the King of kings. Which are you most hungry for?

Turn the World Upside Down

Acts 17:6

Today's Phrase: I'm old enough to remember the *Ed Sullivan Show* and many wonderful Sunday evenings when the family gathered together for his entertaining programs. One particularly vivid memory was Mr. Sullivan's bold unveiling of the Liverpool four known as the Beatles. After that initial exposure, the media coined the term "Beatlemania"; and I, along with millions of other teens, joined in the "rock and roll" revolution. In the ensuing years, group after group poured out from England's shores. But for me and countless others, it was that first *Ed Sullivan Show* and the Beatles that "turned the world upside down."

The book of Acts records the origin of the phrase "turn the world upside down," but the revolution was quite different in that day.

Biblical Background: Acts 17 opens as Paul is teaching in the Jewish synagogue at Thessalonica: "And Paul, as his manner was, went in unto them, and three sabbath days reasoned with them out of the scriptures" (Acts 17:2). Some believed, and some rejected Paul's teachings.

"But the Jews which believed not, moved with envy, took unto them certain lewd fellows of the baser sort, and gathered a company, and set all the city on an uproar" (Acts 17:5).

A mob had been assembled; and now they made ready an assault on the house of Jason, a believer who apparently was boarding Paul and other ministers in his home.

"And (they) assaulted the house of Jason, and sought to bring them out to the people. And when they found them not, they drew Jason and certain brethren unto the rulers of the city, crying, These that have turned the world upside down are come hither also" (Acts 17:5–6).

The mob delivered Jason and his household to the Roman rulers, charging that Paul's preaching of Jesus was "turning the world upside down." Jason was fined and released, but the "revolution" had begun.

Bible Byte: My "rock and roll" days have long since faded, and so have the Beatles. They had a profound effect on the music of their day, but their original songs are now mere "golden oldies" for today's youth.

Paul's revolution, however, has spanned the centuries. It lives on yet today. The power of Christ to convert the sinner will always have profound impact on the lives of individuals. Is your world out of order? Permit Christ to make an impact. He'll "turn your world upside down." Fortunately, with Christ, all things are right side up.

Writing Is on the Wall

Daniel 5:25–31

Today's Phrase: "The writing is on the wall" is an extremely popular expression. It's heard in business and in casual conversation, but it's probably most familiar as a foreteller of doom to the sports fan. "Bottom of the ninth … two out … full count … Cubs trail 10–0 … fans, the writing is on the wall." It also relates to a fascinating defeat recorded in the Old Testament book of Daniel.

Biblical Background: Chapter 5 begins with the new king of Babylon, Belshazzar, commissioning a great feast. Belshazzar ascended to the throne sometime after Nebuchadnezzar.

"Belshazzar the king made a great feast to a thousand of his lords, and drank wine before the thousand" (Daniel 5:1). Belshazzar's big party got carried away under the influence of alcohol. He commanded that the gold and silver temple vessels taken from the Hebrew captives be brought to the feast so that his party guests might drink from them. This brazen act defied the God of Israel and defiled the sacred vessels of temple worship. But apparently, Belshazzar and his guests were too intoxicated to care.

"They drank wine, and praised the gods of gold, and of silver, of brass, of iron, of wood, and of stone" (Daniel 5:4). However, God directly intervened in this open act of defiance: "In the same hour came forth fingers of a man's hand, and wrote over against the candlestick upon the plaister of the wall of the king's palace: and the king saw the part of the hand that wrote" (Daniel 5:5).

Belshazzar may have been drunk, but at this shocking vision, his knees were shaking: "Then the king's countenance was changed, and his thoughts troubled him, so that the joints of his loins were loosed, and his knees smote one against another" (Daniel 5:6).

He called for his wise men and astrologers, promising great reward to anyone able to read the writing and interpret it: "Then came in all the king's wise men: but they could not read the writing, nor make known to the king the interpretation thereof" (Daniel 5:8).

Again, Belshazzar was greatly troubled. His queen remembered Daniel, a captive Jew, who had sometime before demonstrated a special talent for interpreting Nebuchadnezzar's perplexing dreams. Daniel was called, and he consented to read and interpret the writing on the wall. But he also boldly upbraided Belshazzar for defiling, insulting, and mocking the God of Israel. Following his bold statements, Daniel confidently read and interpreted the writing: "And this is the writing that was written, MENE, MENE, TEKEL, UPHARSIN. This is the interpretation of the thing: MENE; God hath numbered thy kingdom, and finished it. TEKEL; Thou art weighed in the balances, and art found wanting. PERES [singular form of Upharsin]; Thy kingdom is divided, and given to the Medes and Persians" (Daniel 5:25–28).

In other words, Daniel reported to the king that God had numbered Belshazzar's kingdom and that his "number" was up. His kingdom would soon be conquered and divided, overcome by the Medes and Persians. Belshazzar rewarded Daniel with a gold chain, scarlet robe, and a position of prominence in the kingdom; but that was the last act of this doomed party: "In that night was Belshazzar the king of the Chaldeans slain. And Darius the Median took the kingdom" (Daniel 5:30–31).

Bible Byte: Belshazzar's kingdom was defeated. It was doomed, just as foretold by the writing on the wall. Today, this expression is popularly used as the ominous signal of certain defeat. But, another famous sports cliché, coined by Yogi Berra says, "It ain't over 'til it's over." And, fortunately, he's right.

There is still time for you today. Why go down in defeat when victory is within reach? Reach out for Jesus. He fought the fight with Satan and the grave. He won the victory. Claim Christ as your Savior. Without Him, you're doomed to lose. Don't ignore God's writing on the wall.

Written in Stone

Exodus 24:12
Exodus 31:18

Today's Phrase: To perfectionists, there's only one way to do anything—their way. And perfectionists can be pretty annoying. I should know. My wife has told me often enough. Actually, she has helped me back off from my previously overbearing pickiness, but I can well remember her frequent challenge: "Where is it written in stone that I have to do it your way?"

"Written in stone" is a familiar saying, synonymous with ultimate authority. We've adapted the phrase to our modern culture and have even developed a modern variation: "written in concrete." The meaning is the same. It originates from ancient scriptural history and God's written law, etched by His finger into two tablets of stone.

Biblical Background: In Exodus 24, Moses is called unto Mount Sinai to commune with God. The children of Israel were left at the mountain's base under the charge of Aaron, Moses's brother.

"And the LORD said unto Moses, Come up to me into the mount, and be there: and I will give thee tables of stone, and a law, and commandments which I have written; that thou mayest teach them" (Exodus 24:12).

Moses remained on the mountain for forty days and nights, receiving God's instruction. The laws of God, known as the Ten Commandments, were given to Moses: "And he gave unto Moses, when he had made an end of communing with him upon mount Sinai, two tables of testimony, tables of stone, written with the finger of God" (Exodus 31:18).

Bible Byte: "Written with the finger of God" … the ultimate authority. Certainly the standard of perfection is reflected in those words, for it was our perfect God who wrote upon the stone tablets. His words represented God's perfect law.

"Where is it written in stone that you should do it my way?" Unless my way is the way of perfection, unless my standards are the ultimate authority, it simply *does not* have to be done my way. And, of course, even though I'm a picky perfectionist, my way is not the standard. God is *the* standard, and no human effort can measure up.

"But we are all as an unclean thing, and all our righteousnesses are as filthy rags" (Isaiah 64:6).

Only Christ fulfilled the law. Only Christ was righteous. Where is it "written in stone"? In God's word, the book of life. Before the final chapter, may your name, too, be written there.

Wolf in Sheep's Clothing

Matthew 10:16

Today's Phrase: A "wolf in sheep's clothing" is a popular phrase synonymous with deceit and treachery. It can be a warning about a business acquaintance, a neighbor, or even a potential date for my teenage daughters. The bottom line is "Don't trust this individual." The phrase originates from Christ's commission to the twelve apostles in Matthew's gospel. Christ described the conditions the apostles were to expect as they went into the nation of Israel to preach.

Biblical Background: It's interesting to note that in this particular chapter of Matthew, the disciples' title is changed to apostle. (Matthew 10:1–2) A disciple is a learner or follower, whereas an apostle is a delegate. These Twelve were now Christ's delegates, going abroad in the countryside to preach. Jesus specifically directed them to preach not to the Gentiles or Samaritans, but only to the "lost sheep of the house of Israel" (Matthew 10:6). Their message was simple.

"And as ye go, preach, saying, The kingdom of heaven is at hand" (Matthew 10:7). It was "at hand" because Christ, the King, was there. There was no need to wait for the Messiah, for the Messiah was in their midst.

Jesus prepared the Twelve for their ministry. He warned they would be scourged, brought before civil authorities, arrested, hated, persecuted, and rejected. Christ cautioned, "Behold, I send you forth as sheep in the midst of wolves: be ye therefore wise as serpents, and harmless as doves" (Matthew 10:16).

Bible Byte: Certainly, the twelve apostles faced danger, and they were warned to be wise. They were sheep in the midst of wolves. But, one among the Twelve may not have been a sheep at all. Judas Iscariot, who ultimately betrayed Christ, was commissioned at this time as one of Christ's twelve apostles. The expression "wolf in sheep's clothing" could very well refer to Judas. He was masquerading as a sheep, but ultimately, was a deceitful, treacherous wolf.

For 2,000 years, the expression has carried a most important warning: There are a lot of "wolves" in the world. Stay close to the shepherd, and you won't be fooled.

Wouldn't Lift a Finger

Matthew 23:4

Today's Phrase: I know several people might consider me a "picky" person. (Six do for sure: my wife and five kids.) I *do* tend to be organized and definitely do not appreciate clutter. In my household, this creates certain conflict. Order can turn to chaos in seconds. My easygoing wife takes it in stride, but it drives me up the wall. The kids have often heard me ranting about this: "You want nice things, but none of you lift a finger to help around here!" I guess I've said that a hundred times, as my mother undoubtedly said to me and her mother to her. In fact, this phrase dates back to Christ's time. He laid the same charge to the scribes and Pharisees. Of course, the clutter they left about was altogether different.

Biblical Background: In Matthew 23, Jesus publicly condemned the Pharisees for their pious and pretentious displays. Jesus's denunciation is tied to another phrase we've previously examined: "Do as I say, not as I do."

"Then spake Jesus to the multitude, and to his disciples, Saying, The scribes and Pharisees sit in Moses' seat: All therefore whatsoever they bid you observe, that observe and do; but do not ye after their works: for they say, and do not. For they bind heavy burdens and grievous to be borne, and lay them on men's shoulders; but they themselves will not move them with one of their fingers" (Matthew 23:1–4).

In other words, Christ blasted the Pharisees for hypocrisy. They put the standard of Mosaic law on the people, yet they themselves couldn't bear it. They enjoyed the distinction offered by their position, while their pretense masked their own sinful condition. They "cluttered" spiritual fellowship with God and "wouldn't" lift a finger" to remove it. Instead, they hid behind their authority and titles. They were called Rabbi, Master, and Father. Yet Christ said in rebuttal, "He that is greatest among you shall be your servant. And whosoever shall exalt himself shall be abased; and he that shall humble himself shall be exalted. (Matthew 23:11–12) Clearly, Christ warned the multitudes to "clean house."

Bible Byte: Is there spiritual "clutter" in your life? If so, remove it. No works you perform will earn salvation. No accomplishments achieved will gain eternal life. We are saved by grace, not works. Ephesians states, "For by grace are ye saved through faith; and that not of yourselves: it is the gift of God: Not of works, lest any man should boast" (Ephesians 2:8–9).

There's a place for good works in the Christian life, but it is not a condition of salvation. Christ denounced this nearly 2,000 years ago. If it's still cluttering up your spiritual house, get the broom out. Lift a finger and sweep it out.

What's Money between Friends?

Genesis 23:15

Today's Phrase: Recently my brother gave me a rather unique birthday present. Knowing I enjoy fossils, dinosaurs, and the like, he purchased a nine-inch-long fossilized tooth from a Tyrannosaurus rex, a vicious, flesh-eating dinosaur. I loved it, but I knew he had paid too much. I quizzed him for details, but he wouldn't tell me. "What's money between friends?" he questioned. "I got it because I love ya." The biblical roots for this popular phrase are contained in Genesis.

Biblical Background: Abraham's beloved wife, Sarah, died at the age of 127 years. She died in Hebron, in the land of Canaan, not in her own dwelling place of Beersheba. Abraham wept in mourning for her.

"And Abraham stood up from before his dead, and spake … I am a stranger and a sojourner with you: give me a possession of a buryingplace with you, that I may bury my dead out of my sight" (Genesis 23:3–4).

Abraham was greatly respected in Hebron. And those he spoke with offered him the choice of any sepulcher in the land. Abraham graciously bowed to these generous people and asked specifically for a cave tomb owned by a man named Ephron, "which is in the end of his field; for as much money as it is worth he shall give [sell] it me for a possession of a buryingplace amongst you" (Genesis 23:9).

But Ephron was not interested in selling the cave. He wanted to *give* it to Abraham, and not only the cave, but also the entire field: "Nay, my lord, hear me: the field give I thee, and the cave that is therein, I give it thee; in the presence of the sons of my people give I it thee: bury thy dead" (Genesis 23:11). Again Abraham bows graciously but insists on paying for the field.

"And Ephron answered Abraham, saying unto him, My lord, hearken unto me: the land is worth four hundred shekels of silver; what is that betwixt me and thee? bury therefore thy dead" (Genesis 23:14–15).

"What is money between us? It's only worth 400 shekels." Abraham insists, however, and eventually pays Ephron the price. But clearly, Ephron's heart was willing, and he did not want money to get in the way of his love and respect for Abraham.

Bible Byte: It's easy to be generous when you know you'll be repaid. Christ taught that even the heathen could be generous if something were in it for them. But Christ challenged men to consider their motives, to be generous without thought of reward. There is a heavy price tag for true friendship. True friendship, true love, requires sacrifice. Are you willing to pay the price? Christ did.

Wash My Hands of It

Matthew 22:24

Today's Phrase: The phrase "wash my hands of it" is commonly used when one tries to separate individual actions from the actions of a group. It could involve anything, from a business meeting to a teenage prank. "I don't want any part of the matter. I'm washing my hands of it."

Pontius Pilate first used this expression, both figuratively and quite literally, before a mob of Jews bent on Christ's crucifixion. Ironically, his symbolic act did not erase his involvement in Christ's death. His actions are permanently etched in the pages of scripture and in the minds of believers the world over.

Biblical Background: Matthew 27 deals with Christ's trial before the Roman governor, Pontius Pilate. Pilate was not at all willing to try Jesus, for he recognized this dispute was a religious matter, not a Roman issue.

As Christ stood before Pilate, he was asked, "Art thou the King of the Jews?" Jesus calmly answered yes, and the Jewish priests and elders began hurling additional charges against the Lord. Christ remained silent, and Pilate marveled. Here stood a perplexed governor. He wanted to please the Jews for political reasons, but he could not find fault with Christ sufficient to impose the death penalty. Pilate, thinking he had an ace in the hole, offered another prisoner, Barabbas, to the people. He wanted to soothe the mob and intended to offer release of one of the two prisoners. He probably thought the mob would release Christ, as Barabbas was guilty of many serious offenses. But the Jewish rulers had incited the crowd to demand the release of Barabbas and the death of Jesus.

"And the governor said, Why, what evil hath he done? But they cried out the more, saying, Let him be crucified. When Pilate saw that he could prevail nothing, but that rather a tumult was made, he took water, and washed his hands before the multitude, saying, I am innocent of the blood of this just person: see ye to it" (Matthew 27:23–24).

Bible Byte: Pontius Pilate recognized the evil of this mob's actions, yet stood by while it occurred. His "clean" hands didn't wash his unclean motives. Today, it is just as convicting to stand idle in the face of wrongdoing. It takes courage to take a stand for God. Clean hands won't open the doors to heaven. Stand up for Jesus. He wants to wash not only your hands but also your whole heart.

Walk on Water

Matthew 14:25
Mark 6:47–49

Today's Phrase: The office is always buzzing when a high-level position is open. The "worker bees" eagerly wait to see which new "star" ascends the corporate ladder. They buzz in the lunchroom, in the hallways, in the restrooms, and at the coffee machine. "It might be Jones over in accounting," someone offers. "No, I heard he resigned from the country club," is countered. "How about Smith in sales? After his record year, he can walk on water."

Even in a secular workplace, most would recognize that this expression has a biblical origin. It's a phrase synonymous with perfection and relates to one of Christ's miracles. Both Matthew's and Mark's gospel accounts describe the event.

Biblical Background: Jesus's popularity was growing among the multitudes from word of His many miracles. After feeding 5,000 men, women, and children from five loaves and two fishes, Christ sent his disciples across the Sea of Galilee toward another village. He remained to commune in prayer with God, the Father.

"And when the evening was come, he was there alone. But the ship was now in the midst of the sea, tossed with waves: for the wind was contrary. And in the fourth watch of the night Jesus went unto them, walking on the sea. And when the disciples saw him walking on the sea, they were troubled, saying, It is a spirit; and they cried out for fear" (Matthew 14:23–25).

Christ spoke to His followers, "Be of good cheer; it is I; be not afraid" (Matthew 14:27). At this, the ever-impulsive Peter responded that if Christ willed it, he, too, could come out on the water to join Jesus.

"And he said, Come. And when Peter was come down out of the ship, he walked on the water, to go to Jesus. But when he saw the wind boisterous, he was afraid; and beginning to sink, he cried, saying, Lord, save me" (Matthew 14:29–30). Immediately, Christ stretched forth His hand and saved Peter.

"O thou of little faith, wherefore didst thou doubt? And when they were come into the ship, the wind ceased. Then they that were in the ship came and worshipped him, saying, Of a truth thou art the Son of God" (Matthew 14:31–33).

Bible Byte: I've always appreciated the scriptural portrait of Peter. From his colorful character, we not only get "Petered out," but now he gives us "Hey, I want to walk on water too." Peter has a very real human character. Like Peter, we want to stick to it but often times weary and "Peter out." Or we get all worked up, believing we can "walk on water"; then realize our own weakness and start to sink. While both may appear to be failures, Peter actually demonstrates his true and very sincere character in both examples. He wept bitterly at his weakness in denying Christ, and he cried out for Christ to save him from sinking. In both instances, he turned from reliance on himself to reliance on God. This is the character Christ saw when he saw Peter, not his personal failings but his ultimate reliance on God.

The corporate world will always have its rising stars. It will also have some falling ones. That's the stuff that keeps the worker bees buzzin'. But show me a guy who "walks on water" and takes his eyes off Christ, and I'll show you a guy who might as well wear cement shoes. Sooner or later, he'll sink, and without God, it will be into a sea of flames.

Whatever Your Heart Desires

Psalm 37:4

Today's Phrase: My children are certainly not bashful about letting Dad know what they want. When those special occasions, holidays, and birthdays roll around, I get inundated with little hints. I like to play dumb, pretending I don't quite grasp their subtlety. Eventually, in exasperation, they say something like, "Dad, don't you wanna know what to get me for my birthday?" "Sure, honey," I reply, "whatever your little heart desires." Psalms has a prescription to ensure receipt of "whatever your heart desires."

Biblical Background: Psalm 37 is written by David. The Psalm opens with an admonition: Don't worry about evildoers, and don't be envious about their prosperity. "For they shall soon be cut down like the grass, and wither as the green herb" (Psalm 37:2).

David also writes of a future promise: "Trust in the LORD, and do good; so shalt thou dwell in the land, and verily thou shalt be fed. Delight thyself also in the LORD: and he shall give thee the desires of thine heart" (Psalm 37:3–4).

David apparently wrestled with the issue of why godless people seem to prosper. Frankly, that's an issue many can relate to today. However, David's words correctly focus not on the "today" of the wicked but upon the ultimate "tomorrow" of the godless.

Bible Byte: Yes, it's difficult to accept the prosperity of unrighteous people. We wonder, "How can God permit that?" But Daniel's psalm says: "Mark the perfect man, and behold the upright: for the end of that man is peace. But the transgressors shall be destroyed together: the end of the wicked shall be cut off" (Psalm 37:37–38).

It may not seem fair now, but God's final judgment will even things out. And, just as I want to give my children the desires of their hearts, God wants to give His children their hearts' desires. As Christ states in Matthew, "Or what man is there of you, whom if his son ask bread, will he give him a stone? Or if he ask a fish, will he give him a serpent? If ye then, being evil, know how to give good gifts unto your children, how much more shall your Father which is in heaven give good things to them that ask him?" (Matthew 7:9–11).

Go ahead; ask the Lord. He wants to give you whatever your heart desires. But don't be concerned with the temporary treasures of this life. Think of things eternal. And let your heart's desire be a heart for God.

Epilogue

What now?

So what now? Even if you agree that the Bible is commonly used in our everyday conversations, so what? In the preface, I stated one of my purposes for writing this work was to promote witnessing. To my shame, however, I've never been very comfortable with a direct witnessing approach. If I'm asked, I'm fine. But I'm very poor at initiating the topic. Some of my discomfort is just personality; some is obviously a lack of confidence or a fear of rejection. But, since I discovered how often people quote the Bible unknowingly, I have developed a very simple and comfortable approach, which many times has led to a genuine witnessing opportunity.

When I hear a casual reference to a phrase that comes from scripture, I can just casually mention, "Do you know where that phrase comes from?"

The exchange that follows can be very superficial, just a casual, friendly response. But, at times, it can be a door opener for a very meaningful spiritual conversation that's comfortable for both of us. Either way, God's word goes forth, some on fertile ground.

You might want to try it. Even if it merely sparks a curiosity that encourages others to read for themselves, it's worth the effort. Remember, we are planting seeds; it's God who gives the increase. Remember, too, that I've not included every colloquial expression that originates from scripture. There are many, many more. Go ahead and search for them yourself. And may God bless you as you read and speak His word.

Bibliography

A Comprehensive Etymological Dictionary of the English Language. Ernest Klein. Amsterdam: Elsevier, 1966.

The Concise Oxford Dictionary of Proverbs. J.A. Simpson and Jennifer Speake, eds. Oxford: Oxford University Press, 1992.

*A Dictionary of Slang and Unconventional Eng*lish. Eric Partridge. New York: Macmillan, 1961.

English Colloquial Idioms. Frederick T. Wood. New York: Macmillan, 1969.

An Etymological Dictionary of Modern English. Ernest Weekly. New York: Dover Publications, 1967.

Heavens To Betsy! & Other Curious Sayings. Charles Earle Funk. New York: HarperCollins, 1955.

Hogs on Ice & Other Curious Expressions. Charles Earle Funk. New York: HarperCollins, 1948.

The Home Book of Quotations, Classical and Modern. Burton Stevenson. New York: Dodd, Mead and Company,1984.

Horse Feathers & Other Curious Words. Charles Earle Funk. New York: HarperCollins, 1958.

Morris Dictionary of Word and Phrase Origins. William and Mary Morris. New York: Harper & Row, 1988.

One Word Leads To Another: A Light History of Words. Milton Paisner.

New York: Dembner Books, 1982.

Stories That Words Tell Us. Elizabeth O'Neill. London: T.C. & E.C. Jack, 1918.

Why You Say It. Webb B. Garrison. New York: Abingdon Press, 1955.

Word Origins and Their Romantic Stories. Wilfred Funk. New York: Bell Publishing Company, 1978.

www.ingramcontent.com/pod-product-compliance
Ingram Content Group UK Ltd.
Pitfield, Milton Keynes, MK11 3LW, UK
UKHW040602210726
13854UKWH00008B/1835